A DISPATCH TO CUSTER
The Tragedy of Lieutenant Kidder

Randy Johnson and Nancy P. Allan
Foreword by John M. Carroll

Mountain Press Publishing Company
1999

Cover painting: "The Kidder Massacre" by David J. Boyle, a gift to the author from Hazel Nordmann

Maps and cavalry insignia drawn by A. J. DeFelice

Library of Congress Cataloging-in-Publication Data

Johnson, Randy, 1945–
    A dispatch to Custer : the tragedy of Lieutenant Kidder / Randy Johnson and Nancy Allan ; foreword by John M. Carroll.
        p.   cm.
    Includes bibliographical references (p.   ) and index.
    ISBN 0-87842-399-0 (pbk. : alk. paper)
    1. Kidder, Lyman Stockwell, 1842–1867.   2. United States. Army. Cavalry, 7th Biography.   3. Indians of North America—Colorado—Wars—1866–1895.   4. Custer, George Armstrong, 1839–1876.
    5. Massacres—Colorado.   I. Allan, Nancy P.   II. Title.
E83.866.K53J63   1999
973.8'1'092—dc21   99-37705
[B]   CIP

PRINTED IN THE UNITED STATES OF AMERICA

MOUNTAIN PRESS PUBLISHING COMPANY
P.O. Box 2399 • Missoula, MT 59806
406-728-1900 • 1-800-234-5308

Dedicated to the memory of Lieutenant Lyman S. Kidder and the men of his command:

Sergeant Oscar Close

Corporal Charles H. Haynes

Private Roger Curry

Private Michael Connell

Private William Floyed

Private Michael Groman

Private William J. Humphries

Private Michael Haley

Private Michael Lawler

Private Charles Teltow

Sioux Scout Red Bead

Died in the performance of their duty on or about July 2, 1867, in combat with Sioux and Cheyenne Indians.

The Kidder Massacre. —Drawing by J. P. Davis, from *My Life on the Plains* by George A. Custer

CONTENTS

LIST OF ILLUSTRATIONS

FOREWORD

Of all the events which constitute a person's biography, there is scarcely one . . . to which the world so easily reconciles itself as to his death.
    —Nathaniel Hawthorne, *The House of Seven Gables*

A biography of Lyman Kidder might be expected to suffer from a lack of detailed and full information, but Randy Johnson and Nancy P. Allan have uncovered more information than was previously known of this man. Students and scholars of the Indian Wars period will applaud the discoveries that support this minibiography. Lieutenant Kidder's death, and only his death, has seared the pages of too few texts, and even then with misinformation that reeks with theatrical prose. Is not his death the only thing most of us know of him?

Randy and Nancy have very successfully destroyed all my misconceptions about the lieutenant. I had always accepted the oft-stated view that Kidder was a new and inexperienced officer from West Point on the frontier, a soldier untried in the art of combat. Wrong! The discovery of his experience in the Civil War, although on the western front, was an eye-opener for me. At the same time of this service, he was involved in the Sioux uprising of 1863, which was certainly a seasoning for a combatant. So his murder, and of those who accompanied him in his ill-fated search for Custer, was an ill-conceived error more than one of supposed "greenness" on the frontier. He was, simply, outnumbered. His command suffered the consequences.

I was most interested in learning that Lyman Kidder had possibly been at a boarding school, where he finished his education. Adding this to the fact that he was in Minnesota with his father at the time, I came up with a possibility. Could he have attended Shattuck Academy at Faribault? This was the academy from which the colorful Tommy Tompkins had graduated. A quick call there found "incomplete records from the 1850s," but I did discover that Lyman's brother Silas had graduated from there, so there is every possibility that Lyman attended Shattuck as well.

The Kidder family papers were a boon to the authors' research, I am certain. For the private letters to have been saved suggests to me that the Kidder family, or at least the patriarch, had a real sense of history. And glad we are that he did. To see this material laid out in book form for the interested reader makes me happy. If I need to know anything about this episode and the actors in the drama, it is all here already written.

I would urge every collector and librarian to consider this book a worthy contribution to their shelves. It adds immeasurably to our knowledge of the western frontier and the military of the nineteenth century. Randy Johnson and Nancy P. Allan deserve a healthy round of applause for adding to our constant demand for this kind of faultless research.

John M. Carroll
Late author and Custer historian

ACKNOWLEDGMENTS

Without the help of the following people this book would not have been possible:

Robert Anderson, Arlington Heights, Illinois

Helen E. Bowen, town clerk, Braintree, Vermont

Bill Boyes, Rockville, Maryland

John M. Carroll, Bryan, Texas (deceased)

Elden and Phyllis Davis, Howell, Michigan

Mary Jo Debes, Barrington Area Library, Barrington, Illinois

Anthony J. DeFelice, Elk Grove Village, Illinois

Steve Erickson, Grand Rapids, Michigan

Dr. Lawrence A. Frost, Monroe, Michigan (deceased)

Linda J. Olmstead-Gagner, genealogical researcher, Rutland, Vermont

Ken Knitig, Goodland, Kansas

Elizabeth B. Knox, New London County Historical Society

Kuhrt family, Goodland, Kansas

Elizabeth Lessard, Manchester Historic Association

John Manion Jr., Beverly Hills, Florida

Jane Pieplow, High Plains Museum, Goodland, Kansas

Michael Pilgrim, National Archives

Lowell Smith, Cullman, Alabama

Marvel Swan, Rutland County Genealogical Research

Judy Telleen, McLean, Virginia

Carol Turchan, Chicago Historical Society

Janet Warren, Goodland Public Library

Carol Kidder Woolfolk, San Jacinto, California

SPECIAL THANKS FROM RANDY JOHNSON:

I would like to thank John Borst and Dayton Canaday of the South Dakota Historical Society for providing Nancy and me with the real inspiration for this book: the Jefferson P. Kidder family papers. Extensive portions of the papers have been quoted herein with the permission of the society.

The site of the massacre is on private property owned by Keith and Judy Coon of Goodland, whom I thank for letting me do my research there. The land where the stone marker of the battle site stands is still owned by the Kuhrt family, though Paul Kuhrt passed away several years ago.

I would also like to thank four very special friends of mine in Goodland. First are Marion and Betty Parker. Marion is a Sherman County historian and the first person I corresponded with when I began my research there. He and his wonderful wife, Betty, have been my gracious hosts on all my visits to Goodland, and I am indebted to them for their help and their friendship. I also thank Marilyn Cooper and Hazel Nordmann for all their help and encouragement in this project. Their knowledge of the people and history of the area was instrumental in the writing of this book.

Finally, thanks to my wife, Jann, for her support.

I

"WHEN THE WATCHWORD
IS VICTORY OR DEATH"

THE HOT KANSAS SUN beat down on the column of weary troops as they plodded along their dust-choked path. These men bore little resemblance to what would later come to be called Custer's Fighting Seventh, the pride of the United States Cavalry. It had been a hard campaign that summer of 1867, with few results save exhaustion and discontent for the men, and frustration and disillusionment for their commander.

The Union Pacific Railroad was laying track through Cheyenne hunting grounds along the Platte River, and General William Tecumseh Sherman, in charge of the Military Division of the Missouri, wanted the workmen protected from resentful Cheyenne warriors. Surveyors had been harassed, a few murdered, and nearly a thousand construction crew laborers had fled to scattered army posts for safety. Some two hundred miles to the south, on the Smoky Hill stage route, Indians had raided the stage stations almost nightly, killing whites and running off horses. Emigrants, too, were streaming westward, many of them in small groups, easy targets for the fast-moving Indians. Sherman planned to use the army to drive the Indians onto reservations north of the Platte, force the emigrants to travel in large caravans on main routes only, and then patrol those routes to prevent attack.

On June 1, Lieutenant Colonel George Armstrong Custer and six troops of the Seventh Cavalry had left Fort Hays, Kansas, with Sherman's instructions "to hunt out and chastise the Cheyennes and that portion of the Sioux who are their allies, between the Smoky Hill and the Platte."[1] Custer was to go north to Fort Sedgwick, on the Platte River, for supplies and further orders, and to report frequently on his progress.

In five weeks and four hundred grueling miles of marching, Custer had been unable to "chastise" the Indians, who fled from his full command but pounced on small detachments. Sioux chief Pawnee Killer, shortly after a parley that included pledges of peace from the Indians and gifts of coffee and sugar from Custer, had surprised the army camp at daybreak and attempted to run off the horses. Fifty of Custer's men

General George A. Custer. —Photo by Mathew Brady, 1865, courtesy Library of Congress

had deserted, some in broad daylight, and the commander's response—ordering pursuers to shoot to kill the deserters—would bring him a court-martial that autumn. Found guilty of this and other charges, Custer was relieved of command for one year.

After setting up camp at the forks of the Republican River, in defiance of his orders Custer sent a wagon train and escort south to Fort Wallace for supplies instead of an equivalent distance north to Fort Sedgwick. It is unknown why he made this decision, but it proved to be a fatal one for twelve unlucky men. Custer then sent Major Joel Elliott to Fort Sedgwick to ask for Sherman's approval of this change and his permission to extend the scout. Elliott took ten men, traveled by night, and returned unscathed. There had been no new orders at Sedgwick, and Sherman could not be reached.

Custer proceeded on his extended scout, and when he arrived at Riverside Station he telegraphed his report. He then learned that new orders had been sent out from Fort Sedgwick on June 29, the day after Elliott's return. The ten-man detail led by Lieutenant Lyman Kidder and accompanied by a friendly Sioux scout, Red Bead, had disappeared without a trace. Custer feared the worst. His own wagons—accompanied by fifty men—had been attacked on the way back from Fort Wallace and the troops had fought off the Indians with difficulty.

Now, on July 12, Custer was anxiously pursuing the trail to Fort Wallace in search of Lieutenant Kidder. The Seventh had taken the trail south at daybreak, with Will Comstock and the Delaware scouts in advance. Shortly after their departure Comstock rode back to report finding the tracks of twelve American horses. As the chief scout had predicted, Kidder had mistaken the trail of Custer's supply train for that of his entire command and had ridden too far south—into the arms of the Indians. Custer later wrote:

> Our day's march was about half completed, when those . . . riding at the head of the column discovered . . . the body of a white horse. . . . It had been shot within the past few days . . . [and] the brand, U.S., proved that it was a government animal.

Major Elliott remembered that while at Fort Sedgwick he had seen one company of cavalry mounted on white horses.[2]

Two miles farther they found the body of a second horse, killed by a bullet and likewise stripped of its equipment. Indians' pony tracks confirmed their fears. Kidder was pursued. Custer later recalled:

We were then moving over a high and level plateau unbroken either by ravines or divides, and just such a locality as would be usually chosen by the Indians for attacking a party of the strength of Kidder's. The Indians could here ride unobstructed and encircle their victims with a continuous line of . . . warriors. . . .

The main trail no longer showed the footprints of Kidder's party, but instead Comstock discovered the tracks of shod horses on the grass, with here and there numerous tracks of ponies, all by their appearance proving that both horses and ponies had been moving at full speed. . . .

We began leaving the high plateau and to descend into a valley through which . . . meandered a small prairie stream known as Beaver Creek. . . . When within a mile of the stream I observed several large buzzards floating lazily in circles through the air. . . .

As if impelled by one thought Comstock, the Delawares, and half-a-dozen officers detached themselves from the column and separating into squads of one or two instituted a search for the cause of our horrible suspicions. After riding in all directions through the rushes and willows . . . one of the Delawares uttered a shout which attracted the attention of the entire command. . . . Hastening, in common with many others of the party, to his side, a sight met our gaze which even at this remote day makes my very blood curdle. Lying in irregular order, and within a very limited circle, were the mangled bodies of poor Kidder and his party, yet so brutally hacked and disfigured as to be beyond recognition save as human beings. . . .

Even the clothes of all the party had been carried away; some of the bodies were lying in beds of ashes, with partly burned fragments of wood near them, showing that the savages had put some of them to death by the terrible tortures of fire. The sinews of the arms and legs had been cut away, the nose of every man hacked off, and the features otherwise defaced so that it would have been scarcely possible for even a relative to recognize a single one of the unfortunate victims. We could not even distinguish the officer from his men. Each body was pierced by from twenty to fifty arrows, and the arrows were found as the savage demons had left them, bristling in the bodies. While the details of that fearful

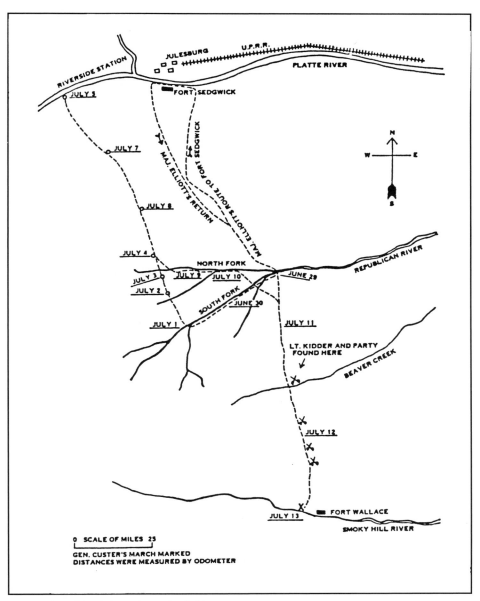

Reproduction of Custer's 1867 field map. —Redrawn from original in collection of Lawrence A. Frost

struggle will probably never be known, telling how long and gallantly this ill-fated little band contended for their lives, yet the surrounding circumstances of ground, empty cartridge shells, and distance from where the attack began, satisfied us that Kidder and his men fought as only brave men fight when the watchword is victory or death.

As the officer, his men, and his no less faithful Indian guide had shared their final dangers together and had met the same dreadful fate at the hands of the same merciless foe, it was but fitting that their remains should be consigned to one common grave. This was accordingly done. A single trench was dug near the spot where they had rendered up their lives upon the altar of duty. Silently, mournfully, their comrades of a brother regiment consigned their mangled remains to mother earth, there to rest undisturbed, as we supposed, until the great day of final review.[3]

The tragic death of Lieutenant Kidder and his men helped convince the army that a new strategy was needed to contain the Indians. The warriors had been attacking small detachments, when the odds were in their favor, rather than facing large bodies of troops. The army decided to strike the Indians when they were most vulnerable, in their winter camps.

In November 1868 Custer and his Seventh Cavalry attacked Cheyenne chief Black Kettle's camp along the Washita River in Oklahoma. In the ensuing battle, over one hundred Indians were killed, including Black Kettle, and fifty-three women and children taken prisoner. The loss to the cavalry was two officers and nineteen enlisted men. (One of the officers killed was Major Joel Elliott, the one whose trail Kidder had followed from Fort Sedgwick to Custer's camp.)

Carrying out this policy, the army won many more victories in the years that followed. Before the turn of the century, the Indian spirit was broken and the struggle was over, at a cost of thousands of lives on both sides.

II

BEGINNINGS

W HO WAS LIEUTENANT LYMAN KIDDER, and what forces brought him to his tragic end on the banks of Beaver Creek, his mission, like his life, incomplete?

He tells us, briefly, in a summary of his life he wrote for the examining board when applying for his commission as second lieutenant, in the spring of the year he was to die.

> I was born at Braintree, Orange County, Vermont, on the 31st day of August, 1842; resided there until 1846 when my father moved to West Randolph in the same county; resided there until 1858 when my father moved to Saint Paul, Ramsey County, Minnesota; and resided there until 1865 when my father removed to Vermillion, Clay County, Dakota Territory, where he now lives. My home has always been with him, except when I was attending school, or in the army. While in St. Paul, I was a clerk in a mercantile house & spent a short time in a printing office.[1]

His family were traditional New Englanders, descended from one Ensign James Kidder of East Grinstead, Sussex, England, who came to Massachusetts about 1650 and settled in Cambridge.[2] Lyman's father, Jefferson Parish Kidder, was the seventh child of Lyman Kidder of Braintree, Vermont, and started life as a farm boy. He attended the Orange County Grammar School, graduated in 1838 from Norwich University (a military college ranking next to West Point in prestige), and served as a teacher and tutor before turning his attention to law. In 1839 he was admitted to the bar, and he practiced law in Braintree and West Randolph. He married Mary Ann Stockwell of Cornwall, Vermont, in 1838. Four children were born to them: Marion Josephine, in 1839; Lyman Stockwell, in 1842; Silas Wright, in 1847; and Jefferson Parish Jr., who lived only three years, in 1856.[3]

Lieutenant Lyman S. Kidder. —Courtesy Minnesota Historical Society

Jefferson Kidder was a delegate to Vermont's constitutional convention in 1843, and from 1843 to 1847 he served as state's attorney. In 1846 he moved his family to West Randolph, Vermont, from Braintree. He served in the state senate from 1847 to 1849, and was granted an honorary master of arts degree by the University of Vermont in 1848.[4] A family genealogy states that he held the rank of colonel in the Vermont state militia about 1850.[5] If the story is true, this was probably young Lyman's first exposure to things military, although Vermont did send a company of volunteers to fight in the Mexican War in 1846.

Lyman was far more likely to have been exposed to politicians, however, than to soldiers. In 1853 and 1854 his father was lieutenant governor of Vermont under Democratic governor John Staniford Robinson. During part of his term Governor Robinson was incapacitated by illness, and Jefferson Kidder performed the gubernatorial functions.

Judge Jefferson P. Kidder. —Courtesy Carol Kidder Woolfolk

In 1857, when Lyman was fifteen, his family moved to St. Paul, the capital of Minnesota Territory and a rapidly growing city of nearly ten thousand.[6] Jefferson Kidder's reasons for moving westward are not known, but he may have felt that politically he had gone as far as he could in Vermont, and it was time to look elsewhere for advancement.

Minnesota Territory in 1857 contained some eighty-five thousand square miles of land on its western border that later became parts of North and South Dakota. Explorations aroused speculators and ordinary citizens alike to the almost limitless possibilities of this vast and largely unsettled land. Proximity to the actual frontier intensified the interest. Government officials in the midwestern border states plunged into real estate schemes they hoped would bring them power and prosperity.

Downtown St. Paul, Minnesota, 1869. —Courtesy Minnesota Historical Society

Jefferson Kidder first rose to prominence in Minnesota in connection with the Dakota Land Company's plan to organize the sparsely settled western frontier into counties, towns, and voting precincts, which existed chiefly on paper. In 1859, one year after Minnesota attained statehood, Kidder was nominated as a delegate to Congress from "that portion of the Territory of Minnesota not included within the limits of the State of Minnesota, now by common consent called Dakota."[7] In spite of his honorable reputation, Kidder apparently was not above practicing a type of political opportunism prevalent on the frontier: he won 1,689 votes from an area some claim was inhabited by barely fifty white men.[8] His opponent, Alpheus G. Fuller, received 147 votes.

The validity of his victory was questioned in Congress, so Kidder went to Washington to fight for his seat. His plea for recognition failed, however, and the judge returned to St. Paul to look for political opportunities there. In 1860 he lost his bid for the Minnesota legislature to Andrew Nessel through a handful of contested votes. (Kidder's tally of votes was 679 to Nessel's 677, but Nessel was seated.)[9] Later he would win and serve two years in the Minnesota House, in 1863 and 1864. He became an associate judge of the Dakota Territory Supreme Court in 1865.

Lyman meanwhile completed his schooling. He does not tell us where, but the statement in his autobiography that his home had always been with his father except when attending school or in the army suggests that during part of his school years he boarded away from home.

In 1861 Lyman Kidder was nineteen, a tall young man at five feet, eleven inches, and handsome, with dark hair and hazel eyes. Minnesota and the Union had need of tall young men in 1861. St. Paul historian J. Fletcher Williams wrote of that unhappy spring:

> The disunion movement . . . steadily advanced, and in its course the depression of business, the failure of banks, and gloomy forebodings of trouble, were the results. In Saint Paul this was especially so. . . .
>
> On April 13, the telegraph brought the sad news of the fall of Sumter, and the call for seventy-five thousand troops.[10]

By July 4, 1861, two Minnesota regiments had already been mustered in at nearby Fort Snelling, and the first had left for Washington. In all, nearly twenty-two thousand Minnesotans joined the Union forces during the Civil War. Among them was Lyman Kidder.

III

"THE NOBLE WORK OF PUTTING DOWN REBELLION"

T HE KIDDERS WERE AN AFFECTIONATE and close-knit family, and
it may have been at his parents' request that Lyman waited until
his nineteenth birthday had passed before obtaining his father's permission to enlist. Jefferson Kidder's letter of permission is dated September
30, 1861, one month after Lyman's birthday, and reads:

> To all whom it may concern:
>
> The bearer, Lyman S. Kidder, is my son & a minor. And I hereby
> give him my consent to enlist into any volunteer military com-
> pany which has been, or is to be organized for the purpose of
> aiding the United States of America in the noble work of putting
> down rebellion and of sustaining the government and the consti-
> tution thereof, and in the protection of the Stars and Stripes.
>
> Jefferson P. Kidder[1]

Lyman Kidder's enlistment papers indicate that he was enrolled
November 1, 1861, at Fort Snelling as a corporal in Company K,
Brackett's Cavalry Battalion, a part of the Fifth Iowa Cavalry. Its captain, Alfred B. Brackett, a resident of St. Paul, was another transplanted
New Englander, born in New Hampshire. From a historical sketch comes
a glimpse of this battalion of volunteers, all set to win glory in a righ-
teous war, despite some imperfections of materiel:

> Under the energetic leadership of Colonel [William W.] Lowe,
> who was a trained soldier of the Regular Army, the regiment became
> quite efficient in drill and discipline before the close of January,
> 1862. The Government was not at that time able to procure the
> best quality of arms for the new regiments, and the "Curtis Horse"
> [the original name of the 5th Iowa Cavalry] was compelled to take

the field with one-half the men armed with the Hall carbine and the old pattern of heavy cavalry saber, and the other half with the Remington revolver and heavy saber.[2]

At the end of November 1861, the Fifth left Fort Snelling for Benton Barracks, Missouri, and from there took the field against the enemy in Kentucky and Tennessee. In a letter to his parents from Fort Heiman, Kentucky, dated August 28, 1862, Kidder told of missing a battle because of illness:

> I have had quite a sick turn for the last eight days. I had been out on a scouting expedition of ten days, with Lt. Neely, and was in the saddle two thirds of the time night and day. Therefore it proved to be too much of a jaunt for me. . . . The rebels marched on Fort Donelson but were repulsed by the 71st Ohio Infantry. Fort Donelson is 15 miles from here and on the opposite side of the river. Col. Lowe ordered our regiment over when the attack was made on the fort. Company K was among those that went. (I being on sick list did not go.) The rebels made a stand about five miles from the fort. The Colonel ordered three companies to charge which they did in good style, but the rebels were concealed behind trees and our cavalry could not get at them. We lost two men killed and eighteen wounded and taken prisoner. . . .
>
> You must excuse me for not writing more but there is so much excitement in camp I can not keep my mind on my work.
>
> Yours with much love, Lyman

Another letter described some of the people in the area where he was stationed:

> I called on an old lady and her daughter yesterday, whom I knew to be strong rebel sympathizers. She said she reckoned we were all Yankees, but had not seen one yet, and when I told her that I was a full blooded Yankee, she was astonished. "Oh Lordy, says she, I supposed you all had ears like a mule." She had been told so.[3]

In the following letter Kidder describes a battle at the Cumberland Iron Works, Fort Donelson, Kentucky, on February 3, 1863:

Dear Mother

I received fathers letter with the stamps yesterday, and now hasten to let you know that I am safe and well as usual. I suppose you have heard of the fight at Donelson. It was quite a battle considering the number engaged. On our side there was six hundred infantry and one battery. The Rebels were under Maj. Gen. Wheeler—Brig's Forrest and Smith—with five thousand cavalry and eleven cannons. They made three charges in order to get into the fort but were repulsed everytime with a heavy loss. We were ordered to reinforce the fort and when about half way between the fort and this place were fired into by the advance guard of five hundred of the rebels sent out on the road to detain us as long as possible in order to give them time to take the fort. All the damage done was to wound one man and a horse killed. We then advanced slowly, feeling our way carefully as we were liable to be fired into at any moment, but such was not to be the case. We arrived at Donelson about 11 o'clock at night, leaving their dead and wounded on the field. On our side the 83 regt. Ill. vol.—lost 10 men. Floods battery—our side had twelve killed and 25 wounded. Our Regt. left the fort twenty four hours after the battle. At that time we had buried 240 dead rebels. Therefore, you see that they suffered terribly. Capt. Von Minden and twenty five of his men were captured four miles from the fort. The men have been exchanged but the Capt. will not be as an order has been issued against by Jeff Davis. Von Minden does not have very good luck, it was the second scout he was ever out on and was captured both times. . . . I have just returned from a short scout in the country having been detailed with five men to go in pursuit of deserters. We went out some thirty miles but could not find them. We lived on the people while out. . . . What is the news about home? . . . I have been detailed as Sergt. of the picket since I commenced this therefore I shall have to close.

> Yours with much Love
> Lyman

On May 18, 1863, Kidder was discharged from the Fifth after being appointed by the governor as a first lieutenant in the First Regiment of Minnesota Mounted Rangers—thanks, no doubt, to his father's influence.[4]

Apart from skirmishes at Paris, Tennessee, and Forts Henry and Donelson, the Fifth Iowa's duties had consisted largely of scouting, protecting the telegraph lines, and preventing the Confederates from recruiting in the neighborhood. Only after Kidder left it did the regiment intensify its operations and wage war on a wider field, serving under Generals Rosecrans, Kilpatrick, and Wilson in the Deep South.

On June 6, 1863, in St. Paul, Kidder joined the Minnesota Mounted Rangers. For the next five months he, like his former regiment, saw heavier service. His enemies were not Confederates, however, but Sioux.

Although the eastern Sioux had ceded most of their land rights in Minnesota to the United States, their presence on reservations within Minnesota's boundaries at midcentury was like a tinderbox awaiting a spark. The spark was lighted at the Lower Agency in the Minnesota River valley, fifteen miles from Fort Ridgely, on August 18, 1862. Indians under Sioux chief Little Crow, angry because their government annuity payment was already five weeks late, exploded in a killing spree against farms and towns in a 50-by-250-mile area of south-central Minnesota. Nearly thirty thousand settlers fled eastward to St. Paul and beyond in the next few weeks, leaving behind them their homes, their possessions, and their dead. Little Crow led 200 to 800 Indians in sorties against Fort Ridgely, where 180 soldiers and 200 refugees staged a gallant and desperate defense.

News of the outbreak reached Fort Snelling on August 19, and fifteen hundred troops under Colonel Henry Hastings Sibley arrived at Fort Ridgely nine days later to break the siege. At the battle of Wood Lake on September 23, Sibley's forces won a decisive victory. Nearly two thousand Sioux were captured or turned themselves in. Many others fled northward with Little Crow to Devil's Lake, near the Canadian border.

The First Regiment of the Minnesota Mounted Rangers was recruited in the fall of 1862 from local citizens, many of whose "wives and children and other relatives . . . had been slaughtered by the barbarous knife and tomahawk."[5] Attacks had occurred within forty-five miles of St. Paul itself. Most of the state was frontier, and this frontier the Rangers patrolled during the winter of 1862–63. When spring came, they joined forces with three thousand men under Sibley—a brigadier general since the Wood Lake battle—in a massive campaign to seek out and punish the remaining Sioux wherever they could be found. Masterminding the plan was General John Pope, sent west after a defeat at Second Manassas to command the newly created Military Department of the Northwest. Another four thousand soldiers under General Alfred Sully were to provide the western jaw of Pope's trap for the Sioux, while Sibley's troops provided the eastern.

*Colonel Henry
H. Sibley.*
—Courtesy Minnesota
Historical Society

The trap was faulty, but its jaws drew blood. Soon after Lyman Kidder's arrival on June 6, the expedition moved west from Fort Snelling to Camp Pope, twenty-five miles beyond Ridgely, then headed northwest on a punishing five-week march to Big Mound, in the central part of present-day North Dakota, where the Indians they were seeking finally appeared in force on July 24. Captain Eugene Wilson describes the ensuing Battle of Big Mound:

> Through the interchange of communications between the scouts the Indians expressed a wish to have a conference. . . . General Sibley . . . having been warned of danger, declined. Dr. Weiser, the chaplain of the Mounted Rangers, however, went among the Indians, many of whom he knew, and returned to the camp saying

that they only wanted peace. He shortly returned to the top of Big Mound with two or three other persons, and was almost immediately shot and killed. His companions escaped by hard riding. . . . As soon as the killing of Dr. Weiser was known General Sibley ordered the First Battalion of the Rangers to attack. . . . Part of the cavalry had to dismount on account of the steepness of the hill, and they fought their way up on foot, driving the Indians before them. A fearful thunderstorm came on during this attack, and it seemed as if offended nature was going to participate and destroy the other combatants. One cavalryman . . . was killed by the lightning. . . . The Indians retreated soon after the first attack, and the cavalry following, a running fight was kept up for some fifteen miles, when darkness put an end to the conflict. It was not till next morning that the cavalry returned from the pursuit. It was difficult to tell how many Indians were killed. Several Indian scalps were taken. . . .

On the 26th of July the savages were again found at Dead Buffalo Lake. After our troops had gone into camp, a large number of them made a dash for some hay cutters and mules.[6]

Lieutenant Colonel William Marshall, commander of the Seventh Minnesota Infantry, singled out Lyman Kidder's charge in the action that followed:

I had but just dismissed the battalion from the color line to pitch tents, when the bold attack of the mounted Indians was made on the teams and animals, in the meadow on the north side of the camp. . . . I assembled and reformed the line, awaiting an attack from the south; but the Indians that appeared on that side quickly withdrew, after they saw the repulse on the north side. . . .

I cannot withhold an expression of my admiration of the gallant style in which the companies of cavalry (I believe Captain Wilson's and Davy's, the latter under Lieutenant [L. S.] Kidder) dashed out to meet the audacious devils, that were very nearly successful in gobbling up the teams and loose animals, that being their object. The Rangers, putting their horses upon the run, were but a few seconds in reaching the Indians, whose quick right-about did not save them from the carbine and pistol shots and saber strokes, that told so well.[7]

Captain Wilson's narrative continues:

Again, at Stony Lake, on the 28th of July, the Indians made an attack. . . . They were mostly mounted warriors, and must have numbered some 2,500. . . .

During this campaign the Indians were tolerably well armed with the trade-gun which they used in killing buffalo and the arms they had taken from troops and settlers. Many still retained the bow and arrows in addition to their guns. At close quarters this was a more dangerous weapon than a revolver. They shot their arrows with great rapidity and precision. Although made of light arrowwood, they were tipped with iron, and given such velocity that they would go clear through a man and show a barb on the other side from its entrance.[8]

Assuredly, Kidder was no stranger to Indian warfare by the end of his service with the Minnesota Mounted Rangers. Nor was he unused to hardships. There had been a drought in 1862, and it continued in 1863. The plains of Dakota were parched and dry, and the troops suffered accordingly. Lieutenant Colonel Marshall, closing his report, wrote, "Soon after the march began, I become so afflicted with irritation of the throat from dust that the surgeon forbade my giving commands to the battalion."[9] Captain Wilson wrote:

The dogs that accompanied the expedition died from thirst, or were shot to prevent their becoming mad. Horses and mules became poor and weak, and many died. . . . A march could not be extended beyond noon, as the rest of the day was necessary to allow the stock to feed on the little grass that could be found. . . . Often on coming into camp the water was found so bad that the troops had to dig wells. . . .

The cavalry, although having the privilege of riding during the march, had really a harder time than the infantry. The latter when in camp had little to do but rest. The . . . cavalryman . . . had to graze his horse during the afternoon and cut grass for his provender at night. When night came he was placed on picket guard on a circle far outside the common camp guard. He was in danger from the wily Indian without and the nervous infantry guard within. Indeed, the habit of having the cavalry guard shot at by the camp guard, under supposition of being an Indian, became so frequent that private instructions were given to return the fire.[10]

And what of General Alfred Sully's four thousand men, who were to have sprung the western jaw of the trap?

> As part of the plan of the campaign, General Sully was to march up the Missouri . . . and be on the other side . . . before General Sibley and the Indians arrived. His transportation of rations and baggage was to be sent by steamboat. The extreme low water in the river, however, so delayed the steamers that he did not arrive in time, and the nicely laid plan to trap the savages failed. . . .
>
> So, after waiting three days and hearing nothing of General Sully, the return march was commenced. The campaign had not proven the success desired, which was the complete destruction of the hostile Sioux. But it was a complete success so far as relieving the State of Minnesota from future attack. The bands that had been located in the western part of the state, and all those east of the Missouri in Dakota, were driven west of that river, never to return. . . . From Big Mound to the crossing of the Missouri their track was strewed by abandoned property; wagons, horses and household goods lined the way. Their tepees were left behind. . . . These, with some of our army wagons that the weakened mules were unable to haul any longer, made a parting bonfire. [11]

Several companies were ordered to return to Fort Ridgely; the main column, Lyman Kidder with it, headed for Fort Abercrombie. Fort Abercrombie's returns for September 1863 indicate that Kidder was with a treaty expedition. In these same returns, under the heading "Record of Events" for September 14, appears the entry, "Ex Gov. Ramsey left here to make a treaty with the Red Lake and Pembina Indians (Chippewas)."

The Chippewa, who earlier had driven most of the Sioux from northern Minnesota, were at peace with the United States in 1863. By the terms of the La Pointe Treaty of 1854, they had ceded areas of valuable timber and mineral resources on the northern shore of Lake Superior to the United States in exchange for annuities and the right to retain permanent residence in the lake area that had been their home. Reservations were set apart for them, and family plots were distributed at the rate of eighty acres for heads of families and forty acres for others. But a large chunk of northwestern Minnesota remained in Chippewa hands. It was for this land, or some of it, that Minnesota senator Alexander Ramsey was sent to treat with the Chippewa bands of Pembina and Red Lake.

Ramsey was an obvious choice; as territorial governor in 1851 he was responsible for the successful negotiation of treaties with the Sioux that opened much of southern Minnesota to settlement. The Old Crossing Treaty—so called because it was signed at the Old Crossing of Red Lake—was concluded October 2, 1863, giving the United States all the rest of present-day Minnesota, except for an irregular portion largely comprising Upper and Lower Red Lake, Lake of the Woods, two state forests, and the Red Lake Indian Reservation. This portion was finally ceded in 1889.

Ramsey was well acquainted with Jefferson Kidder, and he undoubtedly recognized Lyman Kidder among his escort. When the treaty expedition concluded, First Lieutenant Kidder was transferred to Sauk Centre. On November 28 he was discharged from the Minnesota Mounted Rangers at Fort Snelling.

Kidder had dealt with Indians as a soldier in war and in peace. Now he took a nine-month breather from the army, perhaps at his family's urging, and did some clerking; his next enlistment papers, dated August 26, 1864, show his occupation as that of clerk.

For his final stretch of Civil War service, Kidder again chose a company stationed on the Minnesota frontier. This time he received a bounty of two hundred dollars for enlisting as a private in Company E of Major Edwin A. C. Hatch's Independent Cavalry Battalion for a term of two years.

Organized in the late summer of 1863 as a supplemental force to Pope's Indian-fighting army, the Independent Battalion had been sent north to Pembina to protect the frontier settlements from attack by the Sioux just across the Canadian border. During the bitterly cold winter of 1863–64, with temperatures reaching sixty degrees below zero, Hatch's men defeated the Indians at their hunting camp near St. Joseph and captured about four hundred, including two chiefs prominent in the 1862 uprising. The prisoners were taken to Fort Snelling in May 1864, where the chiefs were tried and later hanged. Major Hatch's health had suffered during this campaign to such an extent that he resigned his commission in June while on a leave of absence. Three-fourths of the battalion's horses had died from hunger and cold. Hatch was replaced in September by Lieutenant Colonel C. Powell Adams. Thus, although he spent twenty months in Hatch's battalion, Lyman Kidder never served under its original commander.

On September 1, 1864, one week after his enlistment, Kidder was promoted to first sergeant. If he had hoped for action, he was no doubt disappointed. From this time on, the regimental history indicates merely that the battalion carried on patrol and garrison duties until its companies were mustered out in April, May, and June 1866. Kidder was on furlough in September 1865. In January and February 1866 he was on detached service accompanying prisoners to Fort Snelling—presumably white men. In the Fort Snelling returns for January, February, and March 1866 there is no mention of Indians, but several enlisted men were "in arrest or confinement," and frequent references to court-martials appear under "Official Communications Received." An entry dated February 18, 1866, directs "all enlisted men in Military Prison, St. Louis, to be sent to their commands for punishment." Kidder's prisoners were probably army deserters or malcontents—or just unfortunates who had run afoul of a strict commander. Kidder summed up his service in the Independent Battalion: "I was stationed at Fort Ripley, Sauk Centre, and on the frontier stockade line in Minnesota until May 1st, 1866, when I was discharged at Fort Snelling, Minn."[12]

This time he was not so close to home. Jefferson Kidder, having changed his politics and become a Republican, had been appointed associate justice of the Supreme Court of Dakota Territory by President Lincoln early in 1865 and had moved his family to Vermillion. Lyman joined them and made a "soldier's homestead" on land upon which the University of South Dakota was later erected.[13]

IV

OFFICER'S CALL

LYMAN KIDDER WAS NOT CONTENT to remain a civilian for long. He spent a good part of the last year of his life trying to get back into military service. On October 1, 1866, he wrote President Andrew Johnson, summarizing his wartime record and asking to be appointed "to a First Lieutenancy in some co. in one of the new regiments of cavalry in the reorganized army. Hoping that you will deem it consistent with your duty to give [me] . . . this appointment."[1]

Two highly placed political acquaintances of his father endorsed his application and passed it along to the president. W. A. Burleigh, delegate to Congress from Dakota Territory, wrote from Yankton on October 10:

> I have the honor to transmit the accompanying application for appointment to a Lieutenancy in the Regular Army—and respectfully ask that Mr. Kidder may be appointed—He is a brave and high toned young gentleman, of fine personal appearance—has rendered good service to his country and will prove an honor to the Army.

Alexander Ramsey, governor of Minnesota during the Sioux uprising and then a United States senator, wrote secretary of war Edwin Stanton on October 13:

> Lyman S. Kidder now of the Territory of Dakota was a lieutenant in one of the cavalry regmts. from this state during the late war & as such acquitted himself honorably. Delegate Burleigh has recommended the young gentlemen for appointment as Lieut. in the Regular Army & I write to say that I join in said recommendation.

The winter crawled toward its close while Kidder waited. Finally, on February 8, 1867, there was good news from the War Department:

Your name will be submitted by the President to the Senate for the appointment of second Lieutenant in the 2nd Regt. U.S. Cavalry, in the event of your passing a satisfactory examination as required by the Act of Congress. If you accept this appointment you will at once acknowledge the receipt of this letter to the "Adjutant General, Washington, D.C.," and report for such examination on or before the 20th instant to the Board at Washington, D.C. Upon favorable report by the Board, your nomination will be made. Neglect or failure to notify the Department of your acceptance within ten days from this date, will be treated as declination of the appointment.

W. A. Burleigh responded to the adjutant general on February 15:

I have the honor to state, that I have telegraphed [Lyman S. Kidder] at Saint Paul, Minn., the fact, & his reply thereto states, that he will accept the appointment and that he is now enroute for this city to report in person for examination.

Kidder had written President Johnson in October from Vermillion. The fact that he was in St. Paul that February suggests that he was staying close to rail transportation while waiting to hear from the War Department. His sister Marion was living in St. Paul with her husband, and Kidder may have spent the winter with them. At least, he had made sure Burleigh knew where to find him.

Kidder was in Washington by March 1, upon which date Dr. W. Thomson, assistant surgeon and brevet major, certified him as "physically competent to perform the duties of a Cavalry officer."[2] The written examination was something else. He was instructed at the top of the first page to "Please write, in presence of the Board . . . your name in full, the date and place of your birth, where you have resided . . . and a brief history of your military service, stating the battles, sieges, skirmishes, marches, &c, in which you have participated."[3] Kidder proceeded to fill a page and a half with a fairly well-organized autobiography, misspelling only the word *mercantile*. However, when he answered the first question, "What is the figure of the earth?" with simply "The earth is nearly round," he was already in trouble. On the boundaries of the United States he was better informed than, say, the location of the Mediterranean Sea, which he placed between Italy and Egypt— a far from complete answer, though technically not incorrect. The

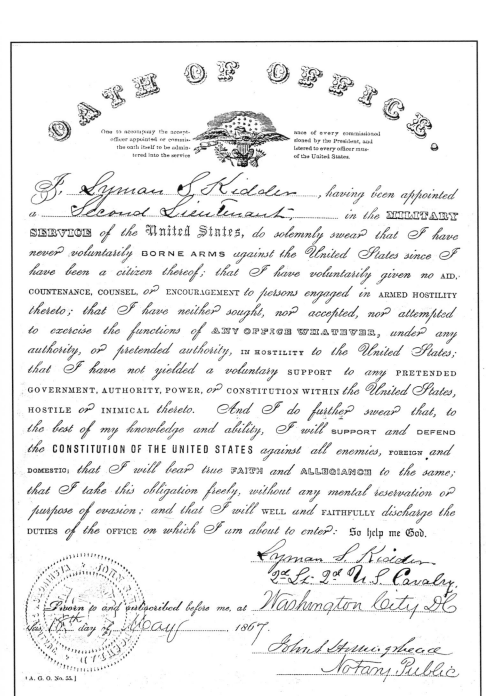

OATH OF OFFICE

One to accompany the accept- officer appointed or commis- the oath itself to be admin- tered into the service

ance of every commissioned sioned by the President, and istered to every officer mus- of the United States.

I, _Lyman S Kidder_, having been appointed a _Second Lieutenant_ in the MILITARY SERVICE of the United States, do solemnly swear that I have never voluntarily BORNE ARMS against the United States since I have been a citizen thereof; that I have voluntarily given no AID, COUNTENANCE, COUNSEL, or ENCOURAGEMENT to persons engaged in ARMED HOSTILITY thereto; that I have neither sought, nor accepted, nor attempted to exercise the functions of ANY OFFICE WHATEVER, under any authority, or pretended authority, IN HOSTILITY to the United States; that I have not yielded a voluntary SUPPORT to any PRETENDED GOVERNMENT, AUTHORITY, POWER, or CONSTITUTION WITHIN the United States, HOSTILE or INIMICAL thereto. And I do further swear that, to the best of my knowledge and ability, I will SUPPORT and DEFEND the CONSTITUTION OF THE UNITED STATES against all enemies, FOREIGN and DOMESTIC; that I will bear true FAITH and ALLEGIANCE to the same; that I take this obligation freely, without any mental reservation or purpose of evasion: and that I will WELL and FAITHFULLY discharge the DUTIES of the OFFICE on which I am about to enter: So help me God.

Lyman S Kidder
2d Lt. 2d U.S. Cavalry.

Sworn to and subscribed before me, at _Washington City DC_ this _8th_ day of _May_ 1867.

John S Hemingshead
Notary Public

[A. G. O. No. 55.]

Lieutenant Kidder's oath of office for appointment to Second U.S. Cavalry.
—Courtesy National Archives

examining board rejected him. Secretary Stanton ordered that he be reexamined on or before March 15. Burleigh wrangled another month's extension.

Kidder was reexamined on April 15. This time, a considerably larger number of the questions dealt with United States geography. He passed. His appointment as second lieutenant, Second U.S. Cavalry, was retroactively dated February 8, 1867. He took his oath of office on May 18, requested thirty days' delay before reporting, and returned home to Vermillion to spend his last leave with his parents. A short article on his departure appeared in the *Yankton Union and Dakotian*, June 15, 1867:

> Lt. Lyman S. Kidder, the popular young officer, has been for a few days visiting his friends at Vermillion.
>
> On June 11th he started for Fort Laramie, the headquarters of his regiment, the 2nd U.S. Cavalry.
>
> His record as an officer in the volunteer service gives promise of a splendid career in the regular army. He will be at his old work fighting Indians. It would be well for the service if there were many more such officers in the army. His numerous friends in the Territory will watch over his course with interest and hope that his promotion will be rapid.[4]

V

"Uncommonly Dear as a Companion and Friend"

Fort Laramie, on the North Platte, was the queen of nine-teenth-century forts and guarded three major trails west: the Oregon, the Mormon, and the Bozeman. In a history of the Second Cavalry, Alfred Bates indicates that Lyman Kidder was originally assigned to Company F, stationed at Laramie, but that on his way to join his company he stopped at Fort Sedgwick.[1] On June 16 he wrote his father:

> I arrived here safely this morning at 6 o'clock. Intend to leave for Laramie at 9 a.m. There has been no Indian difficulty within the last week. I wrote you from Omaha asking for a remittance of $50 to be sent by express to Fort Laramie, D.T. via Omaha. I suppose my sabre has arrived at Sioux City by this time, by express from St. P. If so I would like to have you see that it is forwarded to me.
>
> Love to all,
> Yours affectionately
> Lyman[2]

It is unknown what happened between 6 and 9 A.M. that day to prevent Kidder's leaving. Perhaps someone told him that the Second Cavalry company stationed at Sedgwick, Company M, happened to be in need of a lieutenant and a sudden impulse impelled him to stay. Some days later, Kidder was offered a temporary post there. That he was agreeable to this reassignment was evident in his next letter—and his last—dated twelve days later, June 28:

> My dear Father,
>
> Capt. Mix of the 2d has arrived here with his Co. and as he had no 2d Lt. with him concluded to telegraph to the Comd'g Officer in order to have me assigned to his company. The answer

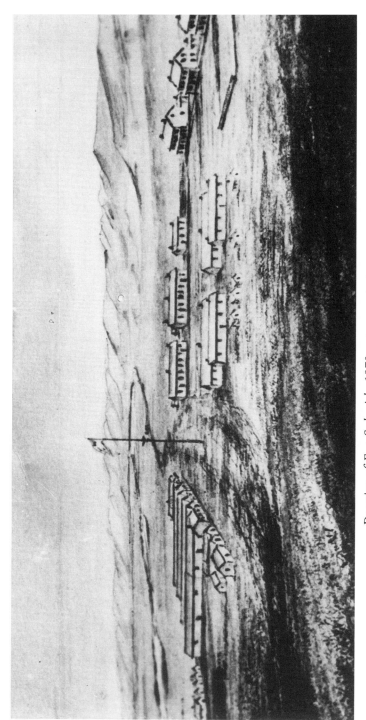

Drawing of Fort Sedgwick, 1870. —Courtesy Colorado Historical Society

to the telegram has been received and I am temporarily attached to his Co.(M). I think it is quite probable we shall get an order in a few days assigning me. I am very much pleased with this Post, from the fact that it is at the terminus of the Railroad. I find the officers of the garrison very agreeable gentlemen. Maj. Cain has treated me very handsomely since I have been here. I room and mess with him.

Major Avery Billings Cain was from Rutland, Vermont, and like Kidder a Civil War veteran. He was twenty-seven years old and had arrived at the post in May. Post surgeon Hiram Latham had spent his early years in West Randolph, Vermont. Kidder may have felt an instant camaraderie with these men, one of whom was from his former hometown. Meanwhile at Laramie, administrators may have been slow to answer Captain Mix's request for his services, which would explain Kidder's delay in writing his father.

His agreeable associates notwithstanding, contemporary descriptions of Fort Sedgwick make Kidder's enthusiasm hard to fathom. William H. Bisbee, stationed at Sedgwick in 1869 with the Twenty-seventh Infantry, called it "a sandy desert of cyclones and rattlesnakes."[3] The fort had started life as an adobe ranch house, which the army purchased from the owner in 1864 and to which the soldiers had added a sod corral and more adobe buildings. General Sherman, visiting the fort in the summer of 1866, was horrified that the army had to live in such squalor. About the only thing that could be said for the buildings was that they were fireproof. But the fort's proximity to the railroad made it an important supply depot for the army. Soldiers from Fort Sedgwick guarded the telegraph lines and offered protection to the Overland Stage and to wagon trains headed west on the Oregon Trail.

Kidder's letter refers briefly to his duties serving on a court-martial. He also speculated on the disposition of the region's Indians:

> The Indians appear to be very quiet about here. However, we do not know how long they will remain so. Gen'l Custer is about 100 miles south of here on the Republican River. It is very difficult to decide as to whether there will be an expedition season. We expect a telegram here today which will decide the matter. If my sabre and the money have been sent, I shall receive them as they have to pass through this office.

The telegram was undoubtedly Sherman's new orders to Custer, which Kidder was to deliver, sending him to his death. It arrived before Kidder mailed the letter to his father, and he added a postscript: "I start for the forks of the Republican tomorrow with ten men. I am to carry dispatches to Gen'l Custer, to be absent 7 days."

Just what was Custer's change of orders that Kidder carried on his ill-fated mission? After General Sherman returned to St. Louis he learned that Custer had sent to Fort Wallace for supplies. Sherman sent an order to Custer through Colonel Henry Litchfield, General Augur's chief of staff at Omaha, stating, "I don't understand about General Custer being on the Republican awaiting provisions from Fort Wallace. If this is so, and all the Indians be gone south, convey to him my orders that he proceed with all his command in search of the Indians toward Fort Wallace and report to General Hancock, who will leave Denver for same place today."[4] Colonel Litchfield transmitted these orders to Colonel Potter at Fort Sedgwick.

Two days earlier, Custer's envoy Major Joel Elliott and his ten-man detail had left Fort Sedgwick and returned to Custer's camp without the expected new orders. Traveling rapidly and at night, Elliott had neither seen any Indians nor been seen by them. Lyman Kidder was not to be so lucky.

Kidder's last orders survive, signed by Lieutenant Colonel J. H. Potter and dated June 29, embellished with many scrolls and flourishes and closing with the archaic courtesy that makes a colonel a lieutenant's "obedient servant," at least on paper:

Headquarters,
Fort Sedgewick [*sic*], C.T.
June 29, 1867.
2nd Lieut. L. S. Kidder
2nd U.S. Cavalry

Sir,

You will proceed at once with an escort of ten (10) men of Company "M" 2nd U.S. Cavalry to the forks of the Republican River, where you will deliver to General Custar [*sic*] the dispatches with which you will be entrusted; should General Custar have left that point you will take his trail and overtake him! After delivering your dispatches return to this post. Until you reach General Custar you will travel as rapidly as possible.

> I am, very respectfully your obedt servt:
> J. H. Potter
> Lieut: Col 30 Infantry
> Bvt. Brig. Gen. USA

The young lieutenant was probably glad to get the assignment. When he left on his last mission, he was no doubt filled with anticipation at meeting the famous general.

Custer's field map of his 1867 scout describes the terrain between Fort Sedgwick and the Republican River as "hard level prairie covered with cactus."[5] We also know that it was broken by ravines; Elliott's detail reportedly concealed themselves in ravines during the daylight hours to avoid detection by Indians. For cavalrymen, even unencumbered by supplies, it was 105 miles of hard riding plus the constant threat of Indian attack.[6]

Writers dealing with the Kidder massacre have asked why Lyman Kidder, a twenty-five-year-old newcomer, was sent on a dangerous scout with ten soldiers, most of whom were younger than himself. As early as 1901, South Dakota historian Doane Robinson made an effort to refute the claim that Kidder was an inexperienced easterner who had never seen an Indian, leading a group of equally untried youths to slaughter. Kidder, Robinson pointed out, "had his military training in five years' volunteer service in the rebellion and Indian wars," and his escort detail "were all strong young men each of whom had seen more than a year of service."[7] They all knew the danger involved; they were ordered and they went. That they did not return was their misfortune, but not necessarily their fault. The army was spread thin on the plains that year, and it faced a rapidly moving and aggrieved enemy.

On June 29 at eleven in the morning, Kidder and his little command departed Fort Sedgwick with Custer's dispatches. Each man was armed with a seven-shot Spencer carbine and a .44-caliber Remington revolver. They took six days' rations and two extra horses. Red Bead, a friendly Sioux who knew the territory, was Kidder's guide.

The men were following Major Elliott's trail back to Custer's camp at the forks of the Republican River, with an approximately

ARMAMENT OF THE KIDDER PARTY
Drawings by A. J. DeFelice

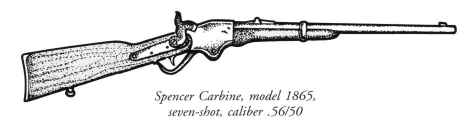

Spencer Carbine, model 1865,
seven-shot, caliber .56/50

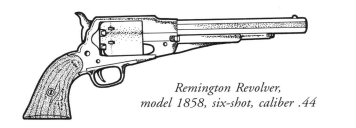

Remington Revolver,
model 1858, six-shot, caliber .44

one-hundred-mile ride ahead of them. The average walking pace of a cavalry mount was about four miles an hour, so they should have made about thirty miles by the end of their first day out. Using this mileage as a guide, one can estimate that they arrived at Custer's campsite in the early evening of July 1. A heavy rain was falling, adding to their disappointment at finding the camp deserted.

They rested at the campsite well into the early morning hours, when the rain clouds began to disappear. Moving out on Custer's heavy trail, the men headed south. The moon was in its cresent, so only a sliver illuminated the dark sky. That may be why Kidder missed the spot where Custer's tracks departed from the main trail, which headed south toward Fort Wallace. Though Custer and his command had marched south after leaving their campsite, they later turned north-northwest toward the Platte River and Riverside Station, some forty miles west of Fort Sedgwick, perhaps to use the telegraph station there. Ironically, Custer's scout, Will Comstock, returning from Fort Wallace on June 27 with Custer's supply train, had reported a trail of warriors going toward Beaver Creek, where Kidder was now headed. Custer would not find the warriors, but the warriors would find Kidder.[8] Kidder and his men seemed to have escaped observation until they were some forty miles south of Custer's camp, four days after leaving Fort Sedgwick. Their confrontation with the Indians most likely took place near midday on July 2.

Years later, stories of their struggle would be told and would not agree. The tracks found by Custer's column indicated a long chase and a "last stand" on ground that was too low to offer protection to the soldiers in their defense. Custer later claimed in *My Life on the Plains* that cartridge shells, in addition to the distance traveled, showed that Kidder and his detail had "fought as only brave men fight when the watchword is victory or death."[9] But in his initial report after finding the bodies, Custer made no reference to a chase:

> Every circumstance seemed to indicate that the Indians had come upon the party at the point where the bodies were found, except the fact that the bodies of two horses, branded "M.2.C." were found about two miles from that point on the trail toward Wallace.[10]

This could mean the Indians found Kidder four or five miles north of Beaver Creek and began a pursuit. Kidder probably ordered the extra horses shot after the chase began so they would not become a hindrance or of use to the Indians. In addition, since the extra supplies were tied to the horses, some of the Indians may have slowed or stopped to inspect and plunder the contents.

About half a mile north of Beaver Creek, the soldiers were forced off the trail by the Indians, veering in a southeasterly direction.[11] It would seem they continued on this path, returning fire whenever possible and yet managing to stay together. From the trail of pistol and carbine ammunition found at the site, a trail that extended over 120 yards, it appears that they were trying to reload their weapons as they rode along, dropping cartridges and fumbling with their guns. At a point about three hundred yards above the creek and still traveling to the east, one of the soldiers was wounded, forcing the column to a halt. At this point they may have spotted the small ravine about a hundred yards below them and decided it was their only hope for a place of defense against the rapidly approaching Indians. All too soon this hope proved vain.

Once they reached the ravine, the men probably grabbed their canteens and extra ammunition and let their horses go. They now found

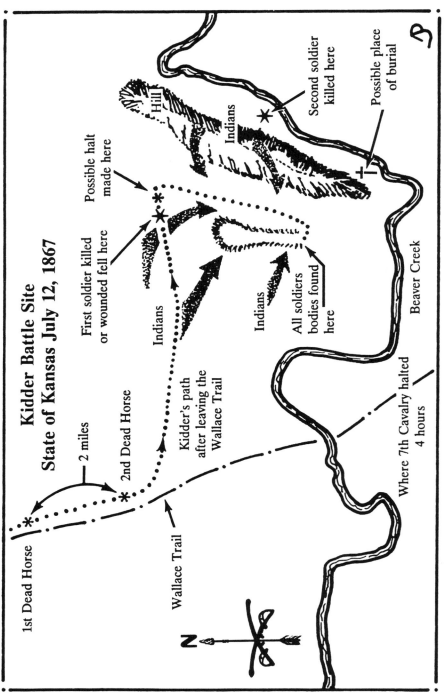

Kidder Battle Site
State of Kansas July 12, 1867

2 miles

1st Dead Horse

2nd Dead Horse

Wallace Trail

Kidder's path after leaving the Wallace Trail

First soldier killed or wounded fell here

Possible halt made here

Indians

Indians

Hill

Indians

Second soldier killed here

Possible place of burial

All soldiers bodies found here

Where 7th Cavalry halted 4 hours

Beaver Creek

N

The Kidder battle site.

themselves in a trenchlike cut in the earth about thirty yards long. Some of the Indians would later describe it as nothing more than a buffalo wallow. The north end was the deepest and widest. In about the center the soldiers could stand and rest their carbine barrels on the edge of the ravine. Each man probably had at least fifty rounds of ammunition, which would have given them well over five hundred rounds for their Spencers. They also had the Remington revolvers. Although they had superior weapons, their field of fire was very limited.

At the time of the battle, the area was covered primarily with prairie grass, making the view at ground level almost completely obscured. Only the bolder mounted Indians who circled the soldiers' position made good targets. As they waited for the warriors' onslaught, the men must have known their situation was hopeless. Each soldier may have silently prayed that death would come swiftly. For at least one unlucky trooper, this prayer would go unanswered.

After the battle, when all resistance from the ravine had ceased, the Indians probably made a rush to finish off any survivors. All the fallen troopers were then dragged from the ravine. At least one soldier was still alive and was put to death by fire. Most of the Indians were armed only with bows and arrows, so the troopers' bodies must have had numerous arrows protruding from them. It would have been necessary for the warriors to dislodge or break off the arrows in the bodies in order to remove their equipment and uniforms.

Custer stated that most of the bodies were found naked, but a few still retained their drawers or shirts. After scalping and mutilating the dead, the Indians shot another twenty to fifty arrows into each body before leaving the field of battle. It seems amazing that they would waste so many arrows in this manner. It could have been an act of sheer contempt or a kind of warning to the army. Like the bodies, the crests of the ravine were bristling with arrows left from the attack. Custer reported that his men picked up hundreds of them.

Theodore Davis, an artist and correspondent for *Harper's Monthly* who accompanied Custer's expedition, stated that Kidder's men had been killed "almost without a fight":

> Very few shots could have been fired by Kidder's party with their carbines, as there were not more than ten or a dozen shells to be found. They may have used their revolvers, but there was every

Discovering the Remains of Lieutenant Kidder and His Men. —Drawing by
T. R. Davis, from *Harper's Weekly*, August 17, 1867

reason to believe that they had been overpowered by the Indians on the first attack.[12]

Did Custer exaggerate the number of cartridge casings found in order to make the army look good, or did Davis have inaccurate information? Breech-loading weapons were new to the Plains Indians in 1867; most of those who possessed firearms were used to the muzzle-loading variety. So the Indians could have picked up numerous empty shell casings as trinkets or curiosities, which would explain the small number found according to the Davis article.

What Indians were responsible? Davis blamed Pawnee Killer's Sioux:

One of the bodies we recognized as that of Red Bead, a friendly Sioux, who had accompanied the party as guide. The body had been scalped, but the hair trophy had not been carried off—a fact that made it certain that the attacking Indians had been Sioux— probably Pawnee Killer and his band. Indians will scalp one of their own tribe who is found with an enemy, but the scalp is invariably left near the body.[13]

Custer originally attributed the deaths to Roman Nose and the Cheyennes, and so he wrote Judge Kidder on August 23. Later he changed his mind and, mentioning Red Bead's scalp, wrote: "The perpetrators of this deed . . . could be none other than the Sioux, led in all probability by Pawnee Killer."[14]

As described by George Bent in a 1906 article, two members of the Indian war party gave a more detailed and perhaps more accurate version of the fight. According to the Indians, a large group of Sioux warriors who had left their camp to hunt buffalo discovered Kidder's men as they approached Beaver Creek. Returning to camp to spread the alarm, the Sioux alerted a dozen or so Cheyennes who were camped nearby. Together they made short work of the Kidder party:

> Tobacco, a Cheyenne leader . . . started to circle the soldiers, and
> the other warriors followed him and opened fire as they rode. The
> Sioux now rode up and threw themselves off their ponies, as Sioux
> nearly always fought on foot. They began crawling in on Kidder's

Indian drawing of the Kidder battle from a Cheyenne warrior's sketchbook recovered by the U.S. Cavalry at the Battle of Summit Springs. —Courtesy Colorado Historical Society

men, firing as they went, while the Cheyennes kept up their cir-
cling . . . All during the engagement the Sioux guide, Red Bead,
kept yelling to the attacking warriors to let him out, but they would
not do it. . . . Two Sioux were killed before the soldiers all fell.[15]

Bent said the Sioux camp was under Pawnee Killer and Bear-Raising-
Mischief, and the Cheyenne under Howling Wolf, Tobacco, and Big
Head—the latter would be taken hostage by Custer in 1869. Two Crows
and Good Bear were Bent's informants. Bent does not mention the
number of the attacking party. Other writers give extravagant guesses,
all the way up to five hundred. Far fewer would have been required to
overcome a fleeing enemy on indefensible ground.

Two letters from Fort Sedgwick to Judge Kidder, both dated July 14,
brought him the first hints of disaster. The first was from Lieutenant
Edward Bailey, a Civil War veteran who had befriended Lyman:

Sioux Chief Pawnee Killer. —Courtesy Nebraska State Historical Society

My dear Sir

I deem it my duty to inform you of the fact that Lieut. L. S. Kidder left this post at about 11 o'c on the 29th ult. [of last month] as bearer of dispatches to Genl Custer, then supposed to be on the Republican River about an hundred and ten miles distant. He was accompanied by a detachment of ten men of Co. M, 2nd Cavalry and two guides [*sic*]. Since leaving here no intelligence has been received from him, tho' Genl Custer was heard from 40 miles west of this Post on Wednesday last, up to which time Lieut. Kidder had not reported to him. When Lieut. Kidder left here it was supposed he would be able to accomplish his mission in the course of a week or ten days at furthest, and his friends are becoming alarmed for his safety. I was commissioned by him, before leaving, in case any accident should befall him to convey to you a knowledge of the facts; but have hesitated until now to write you in the hope that, as day succeeded day, some news from him might reach us. I should be extremely sorry to give you causeless alarm by this communication, but his protracted absence raises in my mind a feeling of apprehension, and I feel that my promise binds me to inform you. I need not tell you how ardently we all hope for his coming, nor indeed have we given him up entirely, there are so many reasons why he might be delayed in the execution of his orders. And be assured I will take the earliest opportunity to inform you of any new facts concerning him.

> I am, Sir, Very Truly,
> E. L. Bailey
> 2nd Lieut.—4th Infantry

The second letter was from Dr. Hiram Latham, the Fort Sedgwick post surgeon:

Dear Sir

I deem it my duty to inform you of the following facts concerning your son Lieut. Kidder, 2nd U.S. Cavy. Upon the 29th day of June he was ordered with ten men to carry dispatches from Gen. Sherman to General Custer, who was encamped at forks of Republican (100) one hundred miles south of this Post. It was thot that he would reach Custer's camp in two days, and rest one day & return in two more. He took an Indian guide & six days provisions. He had ten picked men & two extra horses & besides the guide these men had just been twice over the country. He was

Lieutenant Edward L. Bailey. —Courtesy Massachusetts Commandery
Orders of the Loyal Legion and U.S. Army History Institute, Roger D. Hunt collection

to follow the trail of Maj. Elliot of the 7th Cavy. who had come
from Custer's camp & returned with ten men only (2) days previous & had seen no Indians. Capt. Mix of Lieut. Kidder's Co.
had just returned from a long scout in the same country with
forty men, without seeing a sign of Indians. There was therefore
no thot of danger, although every precaution was taken in arming
& equiping the men. Upon the 5th day of July, Gen. Custer came

to Platte road (40) forty miles above here & had not seen or heard of Lieut. K. Custer had left his camp on the eve. of 29 & made forced marches. In two days time Gen. Custer took up his line of march for Smoky Hill route. Since which time we have not heard from him. Lieut. Kidder has now been out sixteen days & still no news of him. The gravest apprehensions are entertained for his safety. There are no Cavy. here to send for him. If he does not return before the return of M. Co. 2nd Cavy., which is on a scout up Pole Creek, Gen. Potter proposes to go in search of his party. I will give you the earliest information which may be received.

> I am very respectfully your obt. servt.
> Hiram Latham
> Post Surgeon

As the family's uneasiness grew, Silas, Lyman's younger brother, wrote anxiously from Vermillion on July 22:

My Dear Brother

As we have not heard from you since the later part of last month, and as you are in an Indian country where you are exposed to the dangers of the same, we would be pleased to have you write us as often as possible, or at every opportunity, on mother's account as well as our own. We have observed an account of your departure from Ft. Sedgwick on the 29 of June with an escort of ten men and a guide—that you have not been heard from since. Although it appears to be serious, we can not believe the reports to be true. If you have been spared—as we hope and trust you have—although we may be in suspense for several days, we hope you will be careful not to expose yourself to the dangers you are every day subject to.

We all send our love and pray that you may be protected by that divine Providence which has protected us all for so many long years.

> Affectionately,
> S. W. Kidder

The hopes expressed in Silas's letter were shattered with Lieutenant Bailey's next communication to Judge Kidder, dated July 25:

Dear Sir:

Since my last letter to you was written it has been ascertained that our worst fears concerning Lieut. Kidder's fate have been more than realized. It has become my painful task to apprise you of the terrible fact of his overthrow and death, while in the execution of his orders.

It appears, by information from official sources, that Lieut. Kidder's party reached the Republican River at the point where it was expected he would intercept Genl Custer's column, but found it had passed that point, going west, a day or two previous to his arrival. From circumstances, it would seem that Lieut. Kidder discovered that a numerous body of Indians were hovering about the column of General Custer, and even intercepting his line of retreat upon Fort Sedgwick. Finding himself thus placed we infer that he endeavored, by diverging to the south to reach the military post of Fort Wallace, and had succeeded in gaining a point within forty-seven miles of that station when he was overtaken and forced to succumb to superiority of numbers. His body, and those of ten men of his detachment, was discovered by a party from Genl Custer's command and was decently interred. I am not able to furnish any further particulars of this sad occurrence. I may only add, that his brother officers and friends at this Post, from whom his gentlemanly bearing and excellent qualities of head and heart, made apparent during his brief sojourn among them, had won for him their highest respect and esteem, would acquaint you with the knowledge of the heartfelt sorrow entertained by them for the fate of one who had become uncommonly dear as a companion and friend. They would extend to you and the mourners that tender sympathy which can only be felt by those who appreciate, in some degree, the magnitude of the calamity which has befallen you. We mourn the untimely extinction of that young life so lately full of budding promise, quickened with high aspiration, whose silver cord has been thus rudely severed, and be assured, you who have been thus suddenly called to bear this deep affliction, that there are here his late comrades, who feel for you and would bear the weight of this great sorrow with you. Deeply regretting the painful circumstance which makes this communication necessary, I remain, Sir,

Very respectfully, Your obedient Servant,
E. L. Bailey
2d Lieut. 4th Infantry

Marion Kidder White, still living in St. Paul with her husband, Dana, and newly pregnant, wrote to her parents and Silas of their shared anguish:

My very dear Parents & Brother,

Doubtless you were sooner advised than us of the fate of our loved son & Brother. I feel it my duty to write (or to make the attempt) but language is inadequate. You can better understand my heart, so deeply burned, by your own sad experiences. . . . How true it is "death loves a shining mark." . . . And so, "another golden link is broken," but we know it is for our own good, as "he whom the Lord loveth he chasteneth, & scourgeth every son he receiveth." . . . Oh! Mother, I think most of you: whose love is so immeasureless as a mother's. All I am capable of saying is to look to Him who is higher than we: surely there is a balm in Gilead. . . . How comforting it is to think he was permitted to visit you so long his last visit. . . . The time of separation is short. If we live as we should, we shall visit when our final hour arrives. What greater consolation can we ask, to know we shall again meet, no more to be separated, when "God shall wipe all tears from our eyes." . . . I with a prayer wafting upward that you may be made strong, even in sickness,

I am ever your loving
Marion

VI

A Father's Pilgrimage

So Lyman was dead, his life brutally cut off at twenty-five, his body buried somewhere on the treacherous prairie, perhaps beyond reach of his family forever. Jefferson Kidder felt a compelling need to know how his son had met such a death and where his body lay.

He wrote Lieutenant Bailey and Dr. Latham for more information. He would write many letters over the next few months, their urgency couched in formality but nonetheless apparent. The contents of those that have not survived can be guessed at from the replies. From the beginning they had one theme: Jefferson Kidder wanted to bring his son's body home.

Dr. Latham wrote the judge on August 10, 1867. The letter, which included a list of Lyman's effects, gave more details of the tragedy:

Dear Friend

Your letters were received yesterday. I should have written you promptly upon the receipt of official information of your son's fate, but I understood that Lieut. Bailey had done so. I will now give you all the information in our possession relating to this unfortunate expedition. I will say first, however, that upon the arrival of Lieut. K. at this Post enroute to Ft. Laramie I made his acquaintance & we more naturally fell into each others society when we found that we were born & reared in the same valley & had so many acquaintances in common. My impression and the impressions of others were so favorable of your son that, as M co. 2 Cavy was in need of a Lieut. I recommended to Capt. Mix that he telegraph Regt Hdquarters to have him assigned to his co. & as your son was very anxious to stay here, Capt. Mix's request was granted. There had been no Indians in this vicinity for a long time and they had then seemed desirous to steal only, avoiding all fighting in the Platte Valley. Three or four weeks prior to this expedition, Capt. Mix traveled through the whole Republican Valley with forty men & saw no Indians, nor signs of Indians. Ten days prior Gen. Custer started from Ft. McPherson, 100 miles below here, to march to the Republican & traveled up that stream to a point south of this place, & from that place sent Maj. Elliott to this Post with ten men. From McPherson to this Post not an Indian nor an Indian sign was seen. Maj. Elliott returned with the ten men on the 28th. The 29th an escort with dispatches was ordered from here by Gen. Potter. It was thot by all who knew of Indian affairs that it was perfectly safe to go down with the ten men. Lieut. K. was perfectly willing to go with this no. & when he started out we all were sure of seeing him at the end of the five days. His instructions were to take Maj. Elliott's trail & proceed to Gen. Custer's camp. If Gen. C. had moved he was to follow his trail & deliver the dispatches.

Now I must relate events that occurred after Maj. Elliott left Gen. Custer's camp to come to this place. At the same time that Gen. C. sent Maj. Elliott here he sent a train to Ft. Wallace which is 85 miles south of the Forks of the Republican, where Gen. C. was camped, and 190 miles south of this point. I think that he sent a full co. of Cavy with the train. Soon after this departure of the train, Gen. C's camp was surrounded with Indians & one man killed & a bold attempt made to stampede his stock. The same day, the 23rd or 24th, a party of Gen. C's command was attacked 15 or 20 miles from his camp, by 2 or 300 Indians & obliged to retreat to camp for safety. This party numbered 35 & was under command of Capt. Hamilton. About the same time the train before spoken of was attacked on its return from Ft. Wallace, by 4 or 500 Indians & had hard fighting. This body of Indians & the party that fought Capt. Hamilton no doubt were in the immediate vicinity of Gen. C's camp when he moved, which was the morning of the 30th, one day ahead of Lieut. Kidder. Gen. C went directly west up the north fork of the Republican for about 50 miles when he struck north to the Platte.

These hostile Indians, no doubt, hung on the rear & flanks of Gen. C.'s column. When Lieut. K. reached Custer's old camp he no doubt pushed out on his trail & as he had marched for two days over a burning plain with only water at night his men and animals were wearied and worn out and in this condition he must have pushed on right among the Indians. But as he had, as we think, a faithful & sagacious Indian guide who might have given him notice of Indian signs in time to have enabled him to have traveled quite a distance. From the fact that he was found so far south, it is evident that he was cut off from retreat to this Post & when he reached the old camp of Custer's in his retreat he took the trail south just made by Gen. C's wagon train. He must have had a running fight to the point where he was found, from what other point it is impossible [*sic*] to only conjecture. I think that he found the Indians in the vicinity of Gen. C's column which must have been 50 miles at least from the camp, west. And as he was found forty miles from this old camp, I think he fought through 80 or 90 miles. He might, however, have struck Indians at the old camp. I hope soon to know the truth from the friendly Indians, for which purpose I have addressed a letter to the Gov. Interpreter with them. On the ground where they were found there were signs of a desperate fight, but no signs of capture nor torture. The mutilation was the same as usual with Indian victims. I am unable to say whether they were buried in separate graves or not. I will try and ascertain that fact. His watch was with him & also his money, & must have been captured with him. I send a list of his effects, which will be sent to you as soon as the box & $20 is received from Ft. Laramie where it went. It is impossible to tell when he was paid last. The Paym's'tr Gen. can tell. There are no outstanding debts or charges at present. I presume there may be on the money, sword & box, which I will pay & forward bill to you.

——The guide who went out was Red Bead an old Indian who has lived with the whites for years & who is identified with them. His stock was stolen by Indians this summer & his family & all he has in the world are here. It is impossible that he was treacherous. Lieut. K. had ten picked horses & men of the Post, and all the ammunition he could carry & several extra horses. I think it is impracticable to obtain his body at present. I will obtain the address of Comstock, the guide with Gen. Custer when the bodies were found, so that we may obtain all the particulars & have someone who can at any time guide a party to the spot where your son rests. . . . You have the sympathy in your great loss of all who knew your son. All tender their condolence, especially Maj. Cain & myself, who are Vermonters. I remember him as a boy in W. Randolph of 5 or 6 years, and his sister of 9 or 10, at the little white cottage, or on the way to school, hand in hand, she exercising such sisterly care & restraint over him. When I saw him here it immediately reminded me of it.

Anything that I can do for you I will do cheerfully. Hoping that you may be bro't to be resigned to your great loss, and that you will view it as the removing of one more treasure to that country to which we are all so surely traveling.

> I am yours in sympathy,
> H. Latham
> Post Surgeon

Parts of Latham's letter reflected guesswork on his part, and his summary of Custer's movements was not entirely accurate. Custer's report of August 7 stated that his column had moved south on the Wallace Trail for about five miles before taking a right angle to the west for the south forks of the Republican River. Custer wrote that Kidder "probably reached the point at which I left the Wallace trail after dark . . . or before daylight . . . and overlooking my departure from the Wallace trail, continued to follow the latter, hoping to overtake me."[1] The tracks of Custer's wagon train added to the confusion.

That month, Mary Ann Kidder and Silas visited Marion in St. Paul. Soon another sad letter—dated August 18 and probably written in an attempt to cheer—reached the bereaved father.

My very dear Father,

I have been visiting to Aunty this eve, and will try and write a few lines to you. I was very glad to see Mother & Silas, though did not expect them so soon. I had felt so anxious about Mother. She controls herself better than I expected she could. She is very much distressed at times, and feels that her heart is breaking, and that she cannot long survive the shock. Oh, dear Father, it is so hard for us all—you know how hard, you loved Lyman so well. I cannot think of any thing else day or night. Poor, poor Lyman, to think that his dear young life he had to yield up in that dreadful manner, he was so noble. But now his dear aching heart rests beneath the sod, all unconscious of the loved ones who mourn & weep for him. I hope and trust he is at rest in Heaven on high, where all is purity and goodness, gazing down upon those who loved him, with a pure undying love, which only Angels can know. Every one speaks of him in such a praise worthy manner. We have

Marion Kidder White. —Courtesy Carol Kidder Woolfolk

the sympathy of all, but that does not console us in this hour of great trial. . . .

I do hope you can get his loved remains, but I am afraid you cannot unless you go yourself. He has been dead so long I am afraid they cannot be identified. Could we have had but one last look of our beautiful and loved one. Oh, how thankful we would be, but, as it is, it seems we can never realize our great sad loss. Mother thinks she will go back to you in about four weeks. I cannot endure the thought of her going so soon, but she thinks you will be so lonely there alone, and I know you must be. Poor dear Father & Mother, how much I feel for you, how much I wish you could come and make a visit. I think it would do you good. I know the change will do Mother a great deal of good. We are all about as usual. All send love.

> With much love,
> from Marion

Judge Kidder's persistent inquiries brought replies from Lyman's friend and roommate at Fort Sedgwick, Major Avery Cain, and from Lieutenant Colonel Custer at Fort Riley. Cain's letter, dated August 20, was mainly one of condolence, with a little second-guessing about the number of Indians expected to be in the area of Lieutenant Kidder's scout.

Sir,

I am in receipt of two letters from you. Dr. Latham informs me that he has written the particulars of your son's death and enclosed orders recd by Lt. Kidder from Brvt. Brig. Genl. J. H. Potter, Lt. Col. 30 Infy, commanding Ft. Sedgwick. Dr. L—being an interested friend of Genl. Potter had no trouble in obtaining the orders referred to. Lt. Kidder was at this post about two weeks— the 29th June he recd orders from Genl Augur to Genl Custer. Having failed to reach Genl C—he proceeded towards Ft. Wallace Kansas. On account of being attacked by Indians I think he must have had one of the most desperate fights that was ever made as there is but very little doubt but that several hundred Indians attacked him and his small but gallant little band.

At the time your son left here I didn't think it right to send him one hundred miles from the Post with but ten men and an Indian guide especially to the Republican where it was known there were several thousand Indians. Genl Custer had a very good chance the day before your son arrived at the Republican and a few days afterwards to fight them, but he declined and he had about three hundred men at the time. It is not right to send such small parties out a great distance from a Post when it is known that there are several hundred and often times thousands of Indians who are ready to meet and murder them.

Bvt. Brig. General Hunt, Major 4th Infantry, has charge of your son's effects. Genl Hunt is at this Post. I knew you by reputation several years ago having heard my Father speak of you quite often and have seen him address letters to you. I can assure you, Mr. Kidder, that your son's death is very much regretted by the officers at this Post. I became very much attached to him the short time I had the pleasure of knowing him. Lt. Bailey 4th Inf at my request, wrote to you some time ago concerning your son's death.

It cannot but be a very sad blow to you and Mrs. K—. He often spoke of his Father and Mother to me. I don't believe a child ever loved his parents more dearly than your son loved his Father and Mother. He frequently remarked to the officers here that he didn't expect to live until October. Why he made this remark I am unable to say for he always appeared to be in good health. Any other information I can give you I shall be pleased to do so.

> I am very truly
> your friend
> A. B. Cain

Custer's letter was in two parts, the first dated August 23 and the second dated two days later, suggesting that he received another letter from Judge Kidder asking additional questions in the interim.

My Dear Sir

Yours of the 18th inst. [of this month] is just received. In reply I will endeavor to state all the facts and circumstances connected with the finding of your son's remains. He with ten [*sic*] men, one an Indian guide belonging to the Pawnees [*sic*] was sent as bearer of dispatches from Fort Sedgwick to the forks of the Republican river where I was supposed to be encamped with my command. This point is distant from Sedgwick about ninety miles in a S.E. direction. The dispatches of which your son was the bearer were important orders by telegraph from Genl Sherman. Unfortunately, upon the evening of the day of the departure of Lieut. Kidder from Ft. Sedgwick I broke camp and set out upon a lengthened march westward leaving the main southern trail which led to Ft. Wallace and over which a considerable force had passed but twenty four hours previous. I am this minute in detail as it was at this point that your son left my trail and followed the larger trail towards Wallace. In returning from my scout I marched for Ft. Wallace, striking the trail referred to above but a few miles south of the point at which I had left it. I at once discovered the trail of Lt. Kidder and party going towards Wallace, and knowing the dangerous country through which he must pass and the probabilities of his encountering an overwhelming force of savages, I became at once solicitous regarding his fate. The second day after striking his trail we reached Beaver Creek at a point about forty miles north east from Fort Wallace. Here we discovered evidence of a conflict. Two horses which had been recently slain first excited my suspicions. I halted my command and grazed for a few hours, in the meanwhile sending out parties in different directions to discover further evidences of the engagement which had evidently here taken place. The horrible truth of the massacre of your son and his entire party was soon rendered evident. Upon being informed that a number of bodies had been discovered near by, I in company with several of my officers at once visited the spot. There were eleven [*sic*] bodies discovered. This being the number of your son's party, I as well as all the officers with me endeavored to discover or distinguish the body of your son from those of his men. The Indians however had carried off everything which might indicate his rank, and our efforts in this respect were rendered fruitless. I regretted this particularly knowing what a satisfaction it would have been to his parents to have had it in their power to remove his remains at some future time. I caused a grave to be prepared on the spot where the lives of this little band had been given up, and consigned their remains to one common grave.

From the large number of arrows picked up from the ground and from other indications to be observed, it was evident that a desperate struggle had ensued before the Indians were successful in over-powering their victims. It is satisfactorily believed that the party attacking your son was "Roman Nose" and his tribe of Cheyenne warriors, numbering over five hundred warriors. The ground near which the bodies of your son and party lay was thickly strewn with exploded metallic cartridges, showing conclusively that they had defended themselves a long time and most gallantly too, against their murderous enemies. Another proof of the determined gallantry exhibited by your lamented son and his little party was the fact that the bodies, which were probably found as they fell, were lying near each other, thus proving that none had endeavored to flee or escape, but all died nobley fighting to the last. No historian will ever chronicle the heroism which was probably here displayed because no one is left to tell the tale, but from the evidence and circumstances before us we can imagine what determination, what bravery, what heroism must have inspired this devoted little band of martyrs, when, surrounded and assailed by a vastly overwhelming force of blood-thirsty barbarians, they manfully struggled to the last, equally devoid of hope or fear. Believe me Sir, although a stranger to you, and unknown to your son, I deeply sympathize with you and yours in this most sad and lamentable bereavement. And gladly would I tender to the wounds of your afflictions such healing consolation as lies in the power of mortals to give, but I know how weak and futile must my efforts prove. And that in great bereavements like that to which you are now subjected there is but one Power, one Source to which we may hopefully look for that consolation you so much require.

> Very truly yours,
> G. A. Custer
> Bvt. Maj Genl

The second part of the letter continued:

All the bodies found had been scalped and pierced with numerous arrows. As several days had elapsed since the massacre, and as the wolves had disfigured the remains very much it was impossible to determine whether any indignities or barbarities other than scalping had been perpetrated by the Indians. The latter had carried off almost every piece of clothing belonging to our men thereby preventing recognition. Your son was ordered from Fort Sedgwick. Bvt Brig. Genl Potter was at that time comdg that post and undoubtedly is the officer who gave the order you inquire about.

> Very truly yours,
> G. A. Custer
> Bvt Maj Genl

P.S. Upon one of the bodies was a flannel shirt, white with black stripes in each direction. In the pocket of another was a round metallic baggage check, in another was found a printed sutler's check or ticket. These were the only articles found which could by any possibility be the means of identification. If I can serve you in any way please command me.

> G.A.C.

Custer was to write later, in *My Life on the Plains*, that "the marks of a mother's thoughtful affection were to be the means of identifying the remains of her murdered son, even though months had elapsed after his untimely death."[2] Mary Ann Kidder had made Lyman some shirts of black-and-white-checked flannel, which he had taken with him when he left home for the last time. Judge Kidder enclosed a scrap of the checked flannel in another letter to Custer and waited anxiously for a reply. He waited in vain for six weeks. During that time, commanding general of the armies Ulysses S. Grant had ordered Custer to face a court-martial on charges brought by his superior, General Andrew J. Smith, and a disgruntled Seventh Cavalry officer, Captain Robert West. The trial began at Fort Leavenworth, Kansas, on September 15, 1867, and lasted into October. Custer was unable to find time to write Kidder until October 8.

Meanwhile, on August 30, Mary Ann Kidder wrote her husband from St. Paul:

My Dear Husband,

Yours of the 24th inst was yesterday received, being only five days reaching this place. I have thought many times that I would write you & day before yesterday I commenced a letter but was obliged to put it away without finishing. My mind is occupied with but one & the same subject night & day, my precious boy lost & gone forever. There is agony in the thought that I shall never behold his dear face again, never again hear his sweet voice say Mother. . . . Tomorrow would be his birthday & two months yesterday he started out on that terrible fatal journey. Oh what is life that we should desire to live.

I do not think Silas' cough is any better & he has raised fresh blood. Marion went with him two weeks ago to consult Dr. Murphy & Wharton. They examined his lungs & say the disease is in the bronchae tubes & by being very careful he will get over it in a year, but I do not agree with them. I wish I could, but I fear it is incurable. Were it not for Silas' health I should want to remain here until next spring. You will be surprised to know my reason for wishing to stay. Marion is expecting to have an addition to her family & the event will occur in January or early part of February. I regret it very much as I shall feel that I must be with her. . . . I have dear Lyman's photograph & I would like to get one enlarged & painted with a large frame. I hope you will approve of it. If so you will have to send me $25 to meet expenses. I think now that we shall start for Dakota on or about the 17th of Sep't. . . . Please write immediately so that I may have time to get the picture finished. . . . I must close with much love.

M A Kidder

After his brief, unsuccessful attempt to gather firsthand information from Fort Sedgwick, L. H. Litchfield, the U.S. Marshal for Dakota Territory, wrote Judge Kidder from Denver, Colorado, on September 10.

Mary Ann Kidder.
—Courtesy Carol Kidder Woolfolk

Dear Judge

I only had time to stop about one half hour at Sedgwick. Major Cain had gone on a furlough, did not see him. Made inquiries about the boddy only they say he must have been about 300 [?] miles from Sedgwick when he fell consequently they know nothing about the condition of the boddy when found but think that from the length of time they had been exposed that the wolves had entirely destroyed all chances of recognition.

I could not stop longer without stopping two days it being Sunday & no stage on Monday.

Sedgwick is only two miles from Julesburg the present terminus of the UPRR fare from Omaha $40.00.

I will stop a day on my return and find out about the property [Lyman's effects].

In haste
L. H. Litchfield

At last, as his court-martial drew to a close, Custer found time to write Judge Kidder. His letter of October 8 from Fort Leavenworth explodes as myth the commonly accepted story that Judge Kidder traveled to Leavenworth in 1867 to ask Custer's assistance, and that the piece of flannel cloth was agreed upon by them both during that visit as a probable means of identifying Lieutenant Kidder's body.

My dear Sir

Your favor in reply to my last letter came duly in hand, and would have been answered at once but that my time was completely occupied with my trial, now in progress before the General Court Martial assembled here.

I recognized the piece of flannel enclosed in your letter as identical with the shirt found upon one of the bodies, and am satisfied that the body was that of your son. Of this I have not a doubt. In regard to your best course I would suggest that you come from Omaha to this point (Dept Hdqs) from here you can go by Union Pacific Railroad to Fort Hays, which is about two hundred and fifty miles west of here, from F. Hays to Ft. Wallace is about one hundred and fifty miles. Stages run regularly and government trains pass between these posts almost weekly. From Ft. Wallace to the resting place of your son is about forty miles. An escort and transportation could readily be obtained from the Post Commander of Fort Wallace to go with you. Ft. Leavenworth is on your direct route, no other way practicable, being at least one hundred and seventy miles from Platte through an Indian country. I would particularly recommend you stopping here and have no doubt the Dept Commander would extend every facility to aid you in accomplishing your purpose. The Sergeant who prepared the graves &c is now here (Sergeant Connolly of D Co 7th Cav). I would now offer another suggestion for your consideration. From the time elapsed since the interment of the bodies, they must necessarily be in a state of advanced decomposition. In case you are unable to recognize the remains of your son, why not collect those of the entire party. They would occupy but little space, and transport them to the spot intended for your son, surely it would be fitting and appropriate that the noble little band that gave up their lives in one common defence should repose in the same honored grave. I must mention this for your consideration.

I trust and am confident that the restraint I am now under will be removed in a few days and that an honorable acquittal awaits me. When you come I would be glad to render you any assistance in my power.

Believe me

> Truly yours
> G. A. Custer
> Bvt Maj Genl

Now that his pilgrimage was to become a reality, Judge Kidder allowed the pressures of office to force him into a postponement. All during the summer of 1867, in addition to his judicial duties, Kidder had been deeply involved in the organization of the Dakota and Northwestern Railway Company. He was chosen its first president, and along with other incorporators committed personal funds toward a survey of the proposed railroad line, in the hope of receiving a land grant from Congress.[3] This company, the courts at which he presided, and the annual meeting of the Dakota Bar in December combined to appeal to his deep sense of public responsibility and take precedence for a time over his personal needs. But he would also use this time to extend his inquiries and so complete in the most intricate detail all the arrangements necessary for traveling to Fort Wallace and the grave site, and returning home, if God willed it, with Lyman's body. The judge wrote to Custer on October 22, 1867:

> Sir:
>
> Your kind letter in relation to my late son, of the 8th inst., was duly recd., & I am sorry to feel myself under the necessity of further troubling you in the premises. I can't start after his remains until about the middle of December next in consequence of my courts which come in between now & then. Where do you expect to be at that time? Where will Sergeant Connelly who prepared the graves be then? Someone who knows where the grave is should go with me, or I might not find it. Could I be furnished with transportation from Ft. Hays by the government (military) to the place where the bodies are for myself & to return with the remains? Would the Post Commanders be willing to make such an order? or would you? or should I get such an order from Genl Sherman? I want to know how this is, for, altho. I should not hesitate in

relation to the expense if within all I possess on earth if it should come out of me, yet I prefer to know just how it is before I start. I am aware that a box of sufficient size to receive the remains could not conveniently be carried on a common stage coach; so I should be obliged to have an ambulance, or some other transportation than a coach.

Were the skeletons of the men separated at the joints? or were they whole? If separated, I might need a surgeon to find all the parts, even if I could identify the head, or any other part of the body.

If I obtain the remains I intend to remove them to Saint Paul Minn. where some of our relations are buried. Which will be the best Railroad route from Leavenworth, in the winter, to St. Paul?

It will give me great pleasure to hear that you have been honorably acquitted of the charges preferred against you.

I have the honor to be Your obt. Servt.

J. P. Kidder

P.S. I should like to hear from you at your earliest convenience consistent with your personal duties.

J.P.K.

Judge Kidder had also written to General Sherman in St. Louis. In his reply of October 29, Sherman cautioned the judge against having overly high expectations for his trip, while promising to assist him as much as possible.

Dear Sir,

I have the honor to acknowledge the receipt of your letter of October 24, and to say that certainly I will do all that is possible to enable you to secure the remains of your son, who was killed last June near Beaver Creek by the Indians. In order that you may understand all the facts before starting, I enclose you a copy of General Custer's official report, in which you will note that he describes the locality where the remains when discovered were buried, but all the thirteen [sic] skeletons were put in one common grave. Even then, within a month of their death, he could not identify the bones of your son, and expressed the opinion that his nearest relative could not have identified the remains. After the lapse of five or six additional months in a common grave, I doubt if you can distinguish your son. Still, if you propose to try, your best course will be to go to the end of the Kansas Pacific Railroad, now at Fort Hays, of course by rail. There take the regular Denver stage to Fort Wallace, a distance of 140 miles. The commanding officer, on seeing this letter, will give you an escort to the point indicated in General Custer's report; but as it may be better to obtain as guides, one or more of the very men who were with Custer, you had better stop at Fort Harker, and there see General A. J. Smith, or such other officer as commands the District, who will know where to find them. General Custer had with him six companies of the 7th Regular Cavalry, all of which is still serving on that Smoky Hill Line, and I doubt not General Smith will remember the very company that buried the bodies, in which case he will send one or more of them, with an escort, along with you to the graves. He will also order the remains, if identified, to be carried to Ft. Wallace, there carefully boxed and marked and sent to the Railroad at Fort Hays in a Government wagon. From Fort Hayes to your house would require a money order for transportation, and this you had better apply, directly, to the War Department for; and by reciting the fact that I will do all that can be done by means of soldiers and quartermasters wagons, I doubt not the Secretary of War will give an order for transportation and payment by the Government of all the other expenses.

Again tendering you my heartfelt sympathy for the loss of your son, in his early manhood, in so unhappy a manner,

I am, with great respect,

> Yours truly,
> W. T. Sherman
> Lieutenant General

A copy of Custer's August 7 official report was enclosed with Sherman's letter:

I have the honor to report the following facts regarding the finding of the bodies of Lieut. Kidder and party of the 2nd Cavalry. My command reached Beaver Creek forty-seven miles N.W. from Fort Wallace on the 12th ult. I was riding at the head of the column in company with the guide Comstock, and two or three of the Delaware scouts. Upon approaching the vicinity of Beaver Creek a most horrible stench was observable, at the same time numerous vultures or buzzards were to be seen flying in the air. These circumstances added to the fact that the carcasses of three or four

*General William
T. Sherman.*
—Courtesy National
Archives

horses were visible, gave rise to the impression that a fight with
Indians had recently taken place on that ground. I immediately
thought of Lieut. Kidder and party, and would here explain how
he happened to reach Beaver Creek, instead of following me to
the Platte. When Lieut. Kidder left Sedgwick to join me, I was
encamped at the fork of the Republican, on the North bank.

While encamped there my train with a considerable escort was
sent to Wallace for supplies, and had returned making quite a
heavy trail. As soon as my train returned, which it did the same
day Lieut. Kidder left Sedgwick, I broke camp and moved out
about (5) five miles on the Fort Wallace trail intending to follow
up the south bank of the south fork of the Republican. The next
morning I left the Fort Wallace trail, bearing off almost at right
angles to the West. Lieut. Kidder undoubtedly reached my camp

at the fork of the Republican, found I had left, and seeing the trail fresh, followed.

He probably reached the point at which I left the Wallace trail after dark in the evening or before daylight in the morning, and overlooking my departure from the Wallace trail, continued to follow the latter, hoping to overtake me. In no other way can his presence at Beaver Creek, be accounted for. I was made aware of the mistake on my return from the Platte. I struck the Wallace trail again about thirty miles north of Beaver Creek, and it having rained just previous to Lieut. Kidders having passed over it, his trail was easily seen; the guide Comstock determining even the number of his horses.

Impelled by the doubt arising from the suspicious circumstances herein stated, I directed the Delawares to examine the ground in the vicinity of the trail and creek, hoping to discover additional circumstances that would be evidence of the fate of Lieut. Kidder and party. In the meanwhile I moved my command across the creek and prepared to graze and rest. Before completing my dispositions for a halt, one of the Delawares returned and reported the finding of a number of bodies of white men within half a mile of my Camp. Taking a medical officer and a small party with me, I visited the ground and examined closely the bodies of the dead, hoping to be able to identify Lt. Kidder. We found eleven [*sic*] bodies in all.

They had been stripped of nearly all their clothing, a few still retained their drawers or shirts. Ten had been scalped and their skulls broken in the most horrible manner.

The bodies had been so mutilated and disfigured I doubt if the most intimate relative could have recognized any of them.

It was impossible to recognize in any manner the body of Lieut. Kidder. One of the bodies had on a woolen shirt, white with black stripes, running in each direction.

In the pocket of another was found a Sutlers check. Another had a round metallic baggage check. I can give neither the number of check, nor name on Sutlers check, both are in the possession of Lieut. Moylan, Adjt of the 7th Cavalry. One of the bodies was not scalped, at least the scalp remained near the skull as if left undisturbed.

I am now confident that this was the body of the guide Red Bead, as the hair was long and undoubtedly that of an Indian, while the scalp-lock had a brass ring attached about one inch in diameter. My guide Comstock, who knew Red Bead, remarked at the time, that the body was that of an Indian, and the scalp that of Red Bead.

From the relative positions of the bodies and their close proximity to each other as well as the large number of exploded metallic cartridges lying near by. I am convinced that Lt. Kidder and his little band resisted gallantly until the last had fallen. I believe the band of Sioux and Cheyennes that attacked Lt. Robbins and party on the 26 June, numbering over five hundred warriors, was the same that encountered Lieut. Kidder and party.

The latter had evidently taken their stand in a dry ditch or ravine about thirty yards in length and from two to four deep. Unfortunately the ravine was the lowest line of ground in that vicinity and was commanded on all sides by points within arrow-range. The Indians had used the bow and arrow very freely. The crests of the ravine in which Lieut. Kidder and party had fought were all bristling with arrows. Hundreds were picked up from the ground and carried away by my men. The bodies of the slain were thrust full of arrows, their arms and equipment were carried off by the Indians. Three or four horses were killed near where the bodies were lying. Every circumstance seemed to indicate that the Indians had come upon the party at the point where the bodies were found, except the fact that the bodies of two horses, branded "M.2.C." were found about two miles from that point on the trail toward Wallace.

I caused the bodies to be collected and all consigned to one grave. The grave being prepared near the point where they gave up their lives. I have endeavored to state all the facts connected with this most unfortunate affair.

Respectfully submitted
(signed) G. A. Custer
Bvt. Maj. General

The medical officer mentioned in Custer's report was Dr. Isaac T. Coates. When the column reached the massacre site on July 12, Dr. Coates was riding in an ambulance wagon attending three wounded troopers. These men had been pursued and shot down by several Seventh Cavalry officers after they deserted during an afternoon halt on July 7. Custer had ordered that none were to be brought back alive. One of the men, Private Charles Johnson of Company K, after being wounded begged for his life, but was shot again by Lieutenant Cooke.[4] Johnson died of his wounds a few days after the command reached Fort Wallace. Dr. Coates testified at Custer's court-martial that October at Fort Leavenworth.[5]

The starkness of Custer's official report contrasts sharply with his next letter to Judge Kidder, dated November 2, 1867, which offered some encouragement.

Dear Sir

Yours of the 22 ult. came to hand yesterday and it affords me pleasure to be able to furnish you with any information I possess which will serve you. I will reply to your inquiries in the order given by you. I expect to remain at this post [Fort Leavenworth] during the entire winter and spring. Sergeant Connolly [sic] in all probability will remain here also, and I have no doubt the Dept Commander would authorize him to accompany you and assist in identifying the remains of your son. The furnishing you with transportation for Fort Hays and returning is a matter which could be decided by the order of the Department Commander, or the Commanding Officer of the District, and while not authorized to speak for either, I do not hesitate to express the opinion that either of these officers would gladly extend this and all other means of facilitating you in accomplishing the object of your sad journey. Maj. Genl. A. J. Smith Comdg the Dept. in the absence of Genl Sheridan will probably be in command when you arrive here, he left for St. Louis a few days ago to be absent until Saturday. Were he here I would have endeavored to secure from him a promise of the necessary transportation etc. However, I anticipate no difficulty on this score. You can procure a suitable box at Fort Wallace from the Post Commander, to whom I would be pleased to furnish you with introductory letters. If you should happen to see Genl Sherman it would aid you greatly if you were to receive from him a letter of introduction generally to officers whom you may meet in the Dept. This is not absolutely essential, however, as I trust no officer would hesitate or decline to extend all possible assistance in recovering the remains of a brother officer who died gallantly at the post of duty.

The skeletons of one perhaps two of the men were separated at the joints. That, however, which I now believe to have been that of your lamented son was not so separated, but was entire in all its parts. Sgt. Connolly would be of great assistance in this matter and I have no doubt could identify the body. If a medical officer were required, the Post Surgeon at Fort Wallace, I presume, could be made available. I can not advise you as to the best winter route from here to St. Paul. Hoping to see you during the winter, I remain

> Truly yours,
> G. A. Custer

Lieutenant Henry Jackson, the acting engineer officer with Custer's column, added his recollections, which did not entirely agree with those of Custer, in a November 5 letter to Judge Kidder.

Sir

On my return yesterday from the Indian Commission I was handed your letter of the 22nd ult. In answer I would state that the body of your son as near as I can now remember was in the following condition when found—The arms were on the body. The scalp was taken off with nearly all the hair, it had only a little left near the neck at the back of the head. The skull was smashed in. There was a strip of the shirt left round the neck about 3 or 4 inches broad, the rest was torn off. I cannot remember about the legs. I think they were off. The bodies had been so mutilated and dragged about by wolves. The bodies are buried in one grave about 700 yds down the creek from the crossing of the trail from Fort Wallace to the Forks of the Republican on the north side of the creek—about 30 or 40 yds from the creek.

Sergeant Connelly of Company D 7 U S Cav who will be stationed at Fort Leavenworth was the Sergeant of the working party who buried the bodies.

Any other information I can give you in regard to this I shall be only too glad to give.

I remain, Sir

> Yours respectfully
> Henry Jackson
> 1st Lt 7 U S Cav

Sergeant Connelly is positive he can recognize the body of your son.

> H.J.

Lieutenant Jackson was the itinerary officer with Custer's column and had kept a journal of events. The following is his entry for July 12, 1867:

> Left camp 5am course along Capt. West's trail over level prairie covered with cacti to 9 miles 539 yards from camp marked A, where we found a small ravine, then SSW by S to 15 miles 612 yards from camp over rolling prairie to Beaver Creek, which we crossed and halted 4 hours on south bank. . . . Bottom land along narrow valley, grass good, here we found the skeletons of Lt. Kidder and 11 men. They showed signs of having been horribly mutilated, one of them having been burnt. We buried them on the hillside, north of the creek, and about 1/2 mile east of our crossing place.[6]

From Fort Laramie on November 18, 1867, Indian commissioner John Sanborn answered Judge Kidder's query about transportation routes to St. Paul, adding a cautionary note.

> Dear Governor
>
> Your letters of the 22nd, 24th and 29th ultimo have all come to hand. The best route, as I now understand to go to Saint Paul in winter now is by Prairie du Chien, McGregor and the Minnesota Central. You can go all the way by railroad now it is said.
>
> I have had a long talk with Sherman. He cannot pass anybody over the road. If he should be personally present and request a pass for you he could get it. I could do the same with some roads but can do nothing by writing. Sherman told me that he had written you a full statement what he could do and said he would do everything for you that he could.
>
> We have learned nothing yet from any Indian or interpreter about the destruction of that party. When talking for peace we do not like to refer to such events. The interpreters have men who can find out about it I have no doubt. I cannot learn anything of the cash and money yet. But . . . I will make a further effort . . . and will let you know the result.
>
> Sherman says that from the official reports of the condition of the dead bodies of your son's party it will be impossible to recognize the remains of any one in particular. Still I suppose you feel like trying. Certainly I wish you all success, and you can rely upon me to do anything in my power to aid you. Hoping to hear from

you again soon and of your success in recovering the remains of your son, I remain.

> Truly yours
> John B. Sanborn

Judge Kidder must have found Sanborn's reference to peace ironic, reminding him of a part of Dr. Hiram Latham's letter of August 10:

> If there is any blame resting upon any one in sacrificing your son, it is with the Govt. in carrying out such an imbecile policy toward the Indians. Not only your son & his heroic little band have been slaughtered, but hundreds of others, and still the people of the East have not learned that the Indians want war.
>
> Your state, Judge, is disgraced by an Indian com., by name of Sanborn, who prates of laws & rules & decisions as though he was pettifogging a case before a cross roads justice. . . . Such men as Sanborn . . . should be held to answer to this crime of murder.

General Grant's authorization for military assistance in the removal and transporting of Lyman Kidder's body was signed the same day as Sanborn's letter. However, contrary to General Sherman's optimistic assumption, the government declined to assume responsibility for Judge Kidder's expenses.

> Sir,
>
> Your communication of 7th inst. to General Grant, on the subject of recovering the remains of your son Lieut. Kidder, killed by hostile Indians in the neighborhood of Beaver Creek, Kansas, in July last, with a copy of Lieut. General Sherman's letter to you dated Oct. 29, 1867, has been referred to these Headquarters endorsed as follows, which by direction of Lieut. General, I have the honor to transmit for your information. "Respectfully returned to Lieut. General Sherman who is authorized to have through the troops, the body called for recovered and shipped to such point as will enable Gov. Kidder to get it. There is no authority to give the money order asked for."
>
> (signed) U. S. Grant
> Sec of War

Judge Kidder's plans were nearly complete. There remained but to set a date when he could get away and to ensure that someone who knew the route to Beaver Creek would be available at Fort Wallace to guide him. He received the following letter, dated December 9, from Colonel H. C. Bankhead at Fort Wallace:

Sir,

Your letter of the 30th ultimo has just been received. I have questioned Mr. Comstock the Guide at this Post who was present when the remains of your son were found. He informs me there can be no trouble in going from Ft. Wallace to Beaver Creek in January or at any time of the year. Comstock will probably be at this Post and can guide you to the spot where the remains of the party with your son were buried and thinks Lt. Kidder's body can be identified by a shirt which compared with a piece recd by Genl Custer from yourself. I shall be glad to furnish any assistance in my power should I remain at the Post.

> Very Respectfully
> Your Obt Servant
> H. C. Bankhead
> Bvt Col U.S.A.
> Comdg Post

Mr. Comstock informs me that the spot where the remains of the party is buried is 47 miles from this Post. Should you pass Ft. Leavenworth, Depnt Head Quarters, it would be advisable to consult with the Department or District Commander who may, if considered practicable & necessary, authorize an escort be furnished you.

There follows a gap of nearly two months in the collection of letters that tell the story. It is possible that other correspondence took place. At any rate, Jefferson Kidder did not arrive at Fort Wallace until February 22, 1868. He may have stopped en route at Fort Leavenworth, as was suggested to him by Custer and others, but there is no indication that he did so from his remaining letters to his son Silas. He wrote to Silas when he arrived at Fort Wallace:

My dear Son

I arrived here this morning at 3 o'clock in good health but tired riding. The officers will extend to me every facility in their power, several having volunteered to go with me. I shall have an escort of one co. of cav. It is comd. by Capt. Brewster, of St. Paul, whom I well knew. We shall have a train of four wagons, can't travel faster than a walk. It is expected we shall meet Indians, but it is

Silas Kidder.
—Courtesy Carol
Kidder Woolfolk

not expected that we shall have to fight. Still we shall be prepared for the worst; but I pray you, my good boy, don't have any fearful apprehensions in regard to me until you hear from me again.

O, happy sensation! that I am within 47 miles of the remains of dear, dear Lyman, & so soon expect to clasp them in a father's loving embrace. We start tomorrow morning at 7—& expect that it will take us five days, at least, to make the trip. When I return here will at once write you. We intend to bring here all the other bodies & inter them in the military grounds.

All advise me not to go out to Beaver Creek, but stay here & let the military bring in all the bodies; but no money could hire me to stay the while—I might lose some means of identification. Again, I want to see where he so bravely gave up his precious life & where he has slept these long sad months on the ground where he "fought his last battle."

Regards to friends.
Your affectionate
Father

Charles Brewster, a former St. Paul law clerk, had served with Custer in the Shenandoah Valley during the Civil War. In February 1868 he was a first lieutenant and a brevet captain in the Seventh Cavalry. He was with Custer during the 1867 summer campaign and presumably was present when the remains of the Kidder party were discovered and buried.[7] Thus it would have been appropriate that he lead the cavalry escort. However, it was Lieutenant Frederick H. Beecher of the Third Infantry who actually commanded the expedition that recovered the bodies of Lieutenant Kidder and his command.

The same day that Judge Kidder wrote home telling his son of his safe arrival at Fort Wallace and the preparations for his upcoming journey, Lieutenant Beecher also wrote home:

Dear Father:

I am ordered at my request to go out with a party of men in search of the graves of Lt. Kidder and twelve [*sic*] men who were killed last June by Indians. My trip will be some 100 miles. I anticipate nothing that may be unpleasant. I have picked men, good animals and know the country quite well. I hope that I will be successful, for I have with me, a father—Judge Kidder of Dakota—who is very anxious to see where his son was killed, and who wants to take home enough of his remains to make a grave.[8]

The acting assistant surgeon at Fort Wallace, Augustus W. Wiggin, also accompanied the recovery party. He would prepare Lieutenant Kidder's remains for their journey and final resting place in St. Paul.

One person who may not have gone with Judge Kidder's party after all was Will Comstock, the scout. He wrote to the judge from a place called Rose Creek on February 28, 1868:

Dear Sir:

I will do anything sir to help you towards getting the remains of your son. Wait seven days and I will go myself and get them and bring them to you at Fort Wallace. I am on my way to the Arkansas but I will stop and accommodate you as an act of honor after seeing a letter sent to you that I would be here.

Bill Comstock

Did Comstock guide Judge Kidder's party? From the dates on the letters, it is difficult to be sure. Historian John S. Gray contends that Comstock was away from Fort Wallace from January 24 until mid-May

Lieutenant Frederick H. Beecher. —Courtesy Kansas State Historical Society

1868, when Lieutenant Beecher signed him up again as a scout. Comstock had been arrested earlier that January in connection with the shooting death of another man, but upon being freed for lack of evidence he temporarily retired to his ranch.[9]

On February 29, Lieutenant Beecher again wrote home:

Dear Father:

I went out as I told you I intended to and was unsuccessful, owing to a most severe snow storm that covered every sign of a grave. The cold was intense and I have been so suffering from snow blindness since I returned that I can not write. I shall start again today and intend to succeed. I shall wear goggles—a new thing for me. Were it not that I have a father with me who feels the most intense longing to see where a beloved son was killed, I would not endeavor so much.

Finally, on March 5 he wrote of their success:

> I arrived home from my trip with Judge Kidder and brought the remains of his son and ten men [soldiers] who were killed by Indians last year. The sight on the battle ground was terrible. Bones and skulls were scattered in every direction. The poor father had an awful sight to witness. I am quite tired yet, so will not add more.
>
> Your loving son,
Fred

At that time, Beecher was first adjutant and also acting quartermaster of the post. The following September, Beecher left Fort Wallace to serve with General George A. Forsyth as second in command of fifty frontier scouts, a mobile strike force against Indian raiding parties. On the morning of September 17, 1868, the soldiers were attacked by over five hundred Sioux and Cheyenne warriors. Retreating to a small island on the Arickaree River across from their camp, the troopers dug in and a siege began that lasted nine days. Five soldiers were killed and seventeen wounded. Lieutenant Beecher was mortally wounded in one of the first mounted charges by the Indians. Crawling to Forsyth's side, he reportedly said, "General, I have received my death wound." He died several hours later.[10] The fight was subsequently named the Battle of Beecher's Island in his honor.

Now Judge Kidder had completed the most important part of his mission and was back at Fort Wallace preparing to take Lyman's body home. He wrote to Silas on March 6:

> My dear Son
>
> We went out to Beaver Creek, as I last wrote you we expected to, in two days. It is in Colorado [*sic*]. We found the grave at once—had traveled over it when covered with snow. In the morning, exhumed the bodies & found our dear, dear Lyman's almost entire; the most of anyone. I am positive I have his precious remains! The evidence I can state to you when we meet which has caused me to come to this conclusion. It is enough for me to know that I am satisfied. His remains we put into a separate box. The others we brot in with us, & they will all be buried tomorrow morning in one honored common grave under martial orders and religious ceremonies. His body with the assistance of the surgeons I have properly prepared & tenderly "laid out" in the sheet I took

71

from home with me for that purpose & a nice woolen white military blanket & deposited the same in a black walnut coffin as good an one as can be made here—and have put the coffin into a square pine box which is ready for transportation. I would have started today, but for a tempestuous storm which is now raging. The team, a six mule team, will start tomorrow morning with it for the end of the R.R. & an escort of 12 soldiers, which will take about 5 days to reach. I shall start tomorrow eve. & will arrive there in advance of the team. From the time I start on the railroad it will take me 5 or 6 days to reach St. P. only unless I am interrupted. Unless I am delayed you may not expect to hear from me until I arrive at St. Paul. Having rescued our sacred relic! from the burning & barren prairie, the howling wolves & the half open sepulchre, under circumstances that would have deterred almost anyone but a father or mother, my mind goes back to my dear wife & loving children whom I have not heard from since I left, but I pray are well—Dear Marion I have often of late thot of—may she be safe is my constant prayer. When I return to Ft. Hays I shall expect to find letters from all of you.

There is not a house in a 150 miles of here, except what are merely holes in the ground, & except at military posts, nor a cord of wood growing. When we were out in the snow storm, relying on "Buffalo chips" for fuel, the snow covering & wetting them so that they were not fit for use, we had to cut up our wagon boxes for fuel to keep from perishing. I never want to hear any thing more about cold weather, high winds, or scarcity of timber in regard to Dakota. "Bleeding Kansas" beats everything in that direction I ever had any conception of.

Col. Bankhead, the com't of this post sent his wife's remains on a few days since (who died here last summer of cholera) to N.Y. for interment. He expects to go on with me & overtake them at the end of the track.

Write me at St. P. on the receipt of this. . . .

Your most affectionate
Father

P.S. Two soldiers went out from this post last night on special duty & were expected to return in a short time, have not been heard from. It is expected they have frozen. The whole garrison is after them today. I am almost alone & commandant.

VII

HOMECOMING

As JUDGE KIDDER BEGAN HIS LONG JOURNEY toward St. Paul, a letter commending his efforts and recalling Lyman's fight and sacrifice was being composed at Fort Wallace. Cryptically signed only "Soldat" (French for soldier), it has been attributed to Brevet Captain Charles Brewster, who accompanied Judge Kidder and his escort detail to Beaver Creek. The reason the letter was sent anonymously may have been that active army officers were expected to keep their opinions to themselves. The letter appeared in the *Saint Paul Daily Press* on March 18, 1868, the same day as the announcement of Lyman's funeral.

Editors St. Paul Press:

Hon. J. P. Kidder (who will be remembered as a lawyer for many years in your city, and now United States Judge in Dakota) has been out on the plains northwest from here, into the Indian country, accompanied by a military escort from this post, to recover the remains of his son, Lieut. Lyman P. [*sic*] Kidder, of the 2nd United States Cavalry, who was, with ten men of his regiment and a guide, killed by the Indians last July. They returned, being out about nine days, with the remains of the Lieutenant and his men.

Judge Kidder left here last night with the remains of his son, for the purpose of carrying them to St. Paul for interment. The recollection of the manner of the death of this gallant young officer, who was widely known in military circles, having served his country during the entire rebellion, and who was a favorite of all who knew him, is still fresh in the minds of soldiers and others. Lieut. Kidder was bearer of dispatches from Gen. Sherman, from Fort Sedgwick to Gen. Custer, then (supposed to be) in camp at the forks of the Republican river, 110 miles south of the former place, and reached the place to which he was sent in 26 hours from the time he left. Failing to find Gen. Custer, (who left that point the day before) and learning that the Indians had collected in such numbers in his rear—as is supposed, that being true, as since ascertained—that he could not return to Ft. Sedgwick; and still endeavoring, but failing to find Custer on the trackless prairie-sea, the Lieutenant, with a faithful Indian guide, directed his course toward this Fort, when, as interpreters have since learned, his little party was attacked by several hundred hostile Indians. He and his trusty, chosen men, made a brave defense, continuing on their course at such intervals and opportunities as their strategy could procure, saving themselves, but losing some of their horses, (they had three extra ones) for about two days, having fought over 80 miles, and killed more than their own number of Indians. They were, however, about sunrise on the morning of the second of July, over-powered while crossing a low piece of prairie, which was surrounded on all sides by hills. A sudden attack by more than eight hundred savages, brought the party to a stand, here, for decisive resistance. How long and well the band of heroes fought, no tongue was spared to tell! But the copper cartridge "thimbles," or shells (used by them) which were scattered in large quantities on the ground, around their bodies were found, and are still there, are more eloquent than volumes of excitedly written tales. They form a speechful record of bravery and heroism. Interpreters have endeavored to ascertain the number of Indians killed at this point, but have failed to learn the precise number. Although they (the Indians) admitted that they killed "some Indians and wounded fatally some," and that "they (the Lieutenant and party) fought bravely and were not afraid to die."

Lieut. Kidder and his escort will be remembered when many of us who may serve our country longer will have been forgotten.

General Custer, on the 11th of July, when returning to this place with his command, found all their bodies, and buried them on Beaver Creek, Colorado [*sic*], where they were found.

The courage and perseverance which has been exhibited in rescuing the bodies of this brave band from their lone prairie grave, although stimulated by parental affection, is worthy of imitation.

The remains of the enlisted men and of the guide were yesterday buried here in the post cemetery with full military honors and with religious ceremonies.

Action is being taken for the purpose of erecting a suitable monument over their grave.

Soldat.[1]

Two notices announcing Lyman Kidder's funeral appeared in the *Saint Paul Pioneer* on Wednesday, March 18, 1868. Neither Silas nor his mother attended Lyman's funeral; perhaps the family had decided that it would be too difficult for the grieving mother. Dana White, at whose home the services were scheduled, was Marion Kidder's husband.

> The funeral of Lieut. Kidder will take place at the house of Dana White, Esq., at the head of Broadway, tomorrow, the 19th inst., at 3 o'clock P.M. Rev. Mr. Mattocks will officiate. The friends of the family are invited to attend without further notice.
>
> Lyman Kidder's Funeral. —Judge J. P. Kidder arrived home on Monday evening, with the dead body of his son, Lyman S. Kidder, who was killed by the Indians at Beaver Creek, Colorado Territory, last June. Lieut. Kidder was in the 2d U.S. Cavalry, and was inhumanly butchered by the Indians with ten of his men. He formerly lived in St. Paul, and many of our citizens were acquainted with him. His funeral will take place to-morrow afternoon at 3 o'clock.

On March 23, Judge Kidder wrote a final note to Silas on the accomplishment of his mission:

> My dear Son
>
> Yours of the 13th inst. I have recd. here. I arrived here safe on the 16th inst. as I wrote you at Prairie de Chien that I expected to with the remains of dear Lyman! & on the 19th we performed our last sad rite over them in the presence of a large concourse of friends and placed them where his tomb can be watered by the tears of affection. He was buried with full military honors.
>
> You will rejoice with your dear, good mother & myself that success has crowned my efforts, & that I have passed thro. all the perils that attended me in that long, melancholy journey hither without injury.
>
> We expect to leave here Wednesday or Thursday next, stop over at Madison on our old friend Vilas a day or two and arrive in Chicago Saturday, and Wednesday morning of next week start for Vermillion, providence permitting. . . .
>
> Your affectionate
Father

Immersing himself in politics again, Jefferson Kidder became the People's Party candidate for delegate to Congress in the summer of 1868. One of five candidates—among them W. A. Burleigh, who had actually nominated Kidder a few weeks before deciding to run himself—Kidder lost to S. L. Spink in a bitter and vituperative campaign.[2]

In late November 1868, he suffered another, greater loss when his daughter Marion died of typhoid. He wrote Silas from St. Paul on November 28:

> My dear Son
>
>   I arrived here last evening as I expected. I suppose you received a telegram announcing the death of our dear, dear Marion last Monday, after I left. I did not learn of the fatal result until I arrived almost here, altho. I anticipated it as you are well aware. I met a man on the train who told me.
>
>   Yes, that sweet daughter, as pure as the driven snow, is in Heaven, and we should all so live here as to meet her there in a blessed immortality. May the winds be tempered to the shorn lambs. . . .
>
>   Mother sustains herself better, much better, than I anticipated. She is very calm, & does not seem to suffer with grief near as much as when she heard of the death of poor Lyman. I think she will be able to go home anytime when I get ready. You can rejoice with me that your good Mother sustains herself under this terrible affliction so well, I can safely say, that you need not have any fearful apprehensions in regard to her. I telegraphed that I was enroute here, & they preserved her remains—the funeral is to be tomorrow at the Jackson St. M.E. church—she looks perfectly natural, sweet in death as in life.
>
>   My heart is now turned toward you as our only! child. May God in his infinite mercy be a guard around & shield & protect you, & preserve your life, long. Don't get disconsolate, but look at the future on the bright side. I have said nothing yet about returning—shall remain here a week or more. Will let you know when we fix on a time for starting.
>
>   Now, my dear boy, take good care of yourself, & we will be with you—providence permitting—as soon as we reasonably can under the circumstances,
>
> Affectionately,
> Father

Jefferson Kidder was twice reappointed associate justice of the Supreme Court of Dakota Territory by President Grant, in 1869 and 1873. In 1875 and 1877 he was elected to Congress as a Republican.

During that time, tensions had been building between whites and Indians in the West. In the spring of 1868, a treaty had been drawn up between the U.S. military and Sioux and Northern Cheyenne leaders at Fort Laramie, Wyoming, in an attempt to quiet the hostility along the Bozeman Trail, a particular target of Indian aggression. The government agreed to abandon the three forts located on the trail, and the Indians agreed to relinquish their land north of the Platte River. The Indians further agreed to cease committing violence toward whites in the area.

No sooner had the treaty been signed, however, than both sides began to violate it. Hostilities grew, and in 1874 the army sent Lieutenant Colonel George Custer on a thousand-man expedition into the Black Hills. Afterward Custer reported very positively on the area's potential for settlement, and there were even reports of gold there. The government offered to buy the land from the Indians, but they refused, so Congress was forced to consider alternative means of acquiring the land.

On June 29, 1876, four days after the Battle of the Little Bighorn—but before the news reached the public—Jefferson Kidder addressed the House of Representatives to urge the opening of the Black Hills for exploration and settlement:

> Mr. Speaker: On the 28th day of February last, I introduced the following bill:
>
> Be it Enacted by the Senate and House of Representatives of the United States of America in Congress assembled, That all that portion of country in the Territory of Dakota, lying between the forty-third and forty-sixth degrees of north latitude, and the 102d degree of west longitude and the west boundary of the Territory of Dakota, is hereby declared to be open for exploration and settlement; and the true intent and meaning of the treaty with the Sioux Indians, concluded April 29th, 1868, is declared to be that men and women are not excluded, thereby from traveling over, exploring, or settling upon any portion of said territory included within said boundaries.
>
> Sec. 2 That it shall be lawful for any persons to travel upon, over, or through, on foot or otherwise, any Indian Reservation in

said territory, for the purpose of arriving at, going to, or reaching any point or place within the boundaries aforesaid, and returning therefrom in the same manner. . . .

The area of the Sioux reservation in Dakota, including additions, is 56,072 square miles, or 35,896,080 acres. The area of that portion . . . lying west of the 102d degree of west longitude, which includes the Black Hills is 30,636 square miles, which will leave, after this portion is opened for settlement, as a reservation, 25,436 square miles, or 16,279,040 acres. . . .

The number of Indian parties to this treaty . . . is (men, women and children), 40,391. If these lands had been assigned to these Indians in severalty, each Indian, squaw and papoose would have had a title to more than eight hundred and eighty-eight acres. Take from this reservation 30,436 square miles, what this bill calls for, and then there will be reserved for each man, woman and child over four hundred and eighty-two acres; when a white man, including his family, is entitled only to . . . 480. Pass this bill and there is left for each Indian, estimating six in each family, more than five times as much as we are severally entitled to.

Our Government agreed to subsist these Indians, by stipulation in this treaty four years, but since the expiration of that time (1873), it has continued to feed them until up to the time of the making of the report of the secretary of the interior for 1875 it had expended for that purpose $3,395,000. The treaty was never approved by Congress. . . .

It was ratified by the Senate only, and therefore not approved by Congress as the act authorizing the commission to treat with the Indians required it to be; consequently the so-called treaty did not become a law. . . .

This treaty then not having been approved by Congress, the House not having acting upon it, is not only voidable but void, and is not binding upon either party, and before I close these remarks I will try to satisfy you sir, that the Indians, allowing their acts to demonstrate their meaning, so regarded it. . . .

The right of Indians in their land is that of occupancy alone. . . .

The truth is they have never occupied the Black Hills . . . for any purpose whatever, and are now only standing guard at the portal thereof like the "dog in the manger," except that they may also satiate their blood-thirsty appetites in the warm gushing gore of inoffensive victims. . . .

By Article II, among other things, the Indians agreed that "they will not attack any person at home or traveling, nor molest nor disturb any wagon trains, coaches, mules or cattle, of other persons; that they will not attempt to harm white persons, etc." . . .

From the day they fixed their cross to this treaty hitherto they have been engaged in predatory raids upon our frontier, robbing and murdering the white settlers, sparing neither age, nor sex, nor conditions in life, committing "such hellish torture as can only be suggested by savage lust." Hundreds, yes, I may with truthfulness say thousands . . . of our western frontier settlers, whom this Government of ours is bound to protect, have fallen victims to the frightful forays of these barbarians. . . . Miners, wood-choppers, steamboat men and others, have been ruthlessly murdered . . . while in the quiet pursuit of their legitimate business, and our Government at the same time expending millions of dollars annually for the support of these same Sioux. . . . I ask what kind of a claim, if any, have they upon us? I have lived upon the frontier about twenty years, and have had an opportunity to know as much by ocular observation as a man who has never crossed, going westward, the Hudson or Mississippi rivers. Today Sitting Bull and his associate chiefs, who were parties to this treaty, with their 300 warriors, from their strongholds on the Yellowstone and Powder rivers, hundreds of miles from their reservations, shake their bloody girdles of white men's scalps, on some of which the human gore has not yet coagulated, in the faces of your officers, and bid defiance to your laws and military authority.

Sir, in the face of this and more so horrible that it cannot be spoken aloud . . . I would like to know if there can be any obligation, legally or morally, in justice or equity, whereby the "allegiance we owe to God and our country" requires us to adhere to the treaty stipulations. Would we have suffered, unless compelled vie et armis, from any nation such treatment of our citizens? . . . When the pirates from Tripoli outraged our commercial pride, the young nation hesitated not a moment, and demanded and received prompt satisfaction. . . .

We are told to wait until a different policy or a new treaty may enable these Indians to quietly vacate this valuable country; but Young America never waits. It is not the nature of the people of these United States to hesitate to strike the blow while the iron is hot. Remove this dusky cloud's title from a portion of the reservation, and thousands of emigrants will flock there annually, not simply as gold-hunters, but as farmers and tillers of the soil. The climate is temperate and salubrious; the soil is rich; forests abound, and the country is well supplied with small streams abounding in fish. There is no portion of the country that presents so many attractions for the emigrant as this bill proposes to open. The passage of this bill will do the Indians no harm, but will greatly advantage the hardy, whole-souled, generous-hearted pioneers. Pass this bill and this rich country is open for exploration and settlement at once, and gives homes to thousands of the homeless. The interests of humanity demands its passage. It will stop the shedding of innocent blood. Men and women will earn their daily bread in quiet, and after the labors of the day lay down to sleep without fear of being awakened by the yell of the blood-thirsty savage or the glare of the midnight conflagration. The sword will be turned into the plowshare, and "the song of the turtle will be heard in the land."[3]

George W. Kingsbury, in *History of Dakota Territory*, relates the further efforts of Judge Kidder to open the Black Hills to white settlement:

Judge Kidder called upon President Grant, and asked him if there was no possible way for him to use his executive authority to get the coveted country thrown open to white occupation. Grant . . . strongly hinted to Kidder if he could get him authority to appoint commissioners to negotiate with the Indians, and money enough to pay them, he would appoint the commissioners immediately and as speedily as possible make terms with the Indians. . . . [Kidder added a last-minute amendment to an appropriations bill that] authorized the President to appoint commissioners to visit the Sioux country, negotiate with the Indians, and made an appropriation to defray expenses. The amendment was substantially the provision of law which governed in the making of the agreement with the Sioux for the Black Hills, in 1876. The bill passed Congress during August, and in September and October the important agreement was made by which the Indians relinquished all claims to the hills country.[4]

In 1878 Judge Kidder was unable to win a third term in Congress. President Rutherford Hayes appointed him justice of the Supreme Court of Dakota Territory the following year.

On September 29, 1880, Mary Ann Kidder died. Jefferson Kidder had already lost three of his four children to untimely deaths; now he had lost his wife. With only Silas left to him, he devoted even more time and attention to his work.

In the spring of 1881 a group of citizens met in Jefferson Kidder's Vermillion office to establish a university. Appointed president of the board of trustees, Kidder drafted the articles of incorporation. At a later meeting, he donated ten acres of land toward a site—the land that comprised Lyman's homestead. Clay County's records prior to 1881 were washed away by a flood in March and April of that year, but the warranty deed by which Jefferson Kidder transferred the property to the University of Dakota on August 4, 1882, survives. The university opened its doors in October 1882.[5]

In April 1883, Kidder was reappointed judge, but he did not live out his term. Late in September he traveled to St. Paul to have an operation for bladder stones. After the operation, it became apparent that inflammation had set in, and the judge died on the evening of October 2. A postmortem examination disclosed forty-seven stones in his bladder.

The *Saint Paul and Minneapolis Pioneer Press* printed a long biography and tribute on October 3 along with its death notice.

> Jefferson Parish Kidder, an associate justice of the supreme court of Dakota, and judge of the fourth district . . . died at the Merchants hotel at 10:35 last evening, from inflammation of the bladder. . . . The prime cause of the attack was stated by the physicians to have been the failure of Judge Kidder to suspend sessions of his court in order that he might leave the bench when nature demanded. He kept his court in operation from the time it was called until it adjourned—sometimes for six hours without cessation. It may, therefore, be said that in a measure Judge Kidder died a victim to his devotion to his official duties. . . .
>
> His death is looked upon as a personal bereavement by a large part of the people of Southern Dakota, where he had lived for eighteen years, universally respected as a man and an official. Either personally or upon the bench he was most genial and approachable. . . . Even upon the bench he often indulged in jocular remarks, causing a general laugh, and these, he would say, relieved the tedium and kept the machinery of justice oiled. . . . [7]

Silas and three grandchildren survived Jefferson Kidder. The son who had worried Mary Ann Kidder in August 1867 by coughing blood lived on into the twentieth century.

In 1901 Silas donated his father's papers to the South Dakota State Historical Society. Included were all the family's letters at the time of Lyman's death and the voluminous correspondence relating to Judge Kidder's trip to Fort Wallace to bring his son's body back for reburial.

VIII

REMEMBRANCE

L YMAN KIDDER WAS NOT FORGOTTEN, but in the retelling of his final
battle his memory became clouded over with insinuations that he
had been rash, or at least naive. When Doane Robinson told Kidder's
story in the November 1901 *Monthly South Dakotan,* he stated that his
main purpose was to "rescue the memory of a brave young soldier from
a mass of misleading and rhetorical flourishing, with which theatrical
writers have obscured it."[1]

Probably the first of these theatrical writers was Custer, who in his
memoirs put this colorful effusion into the mouth of his scout Will
Comstock during the Seventh Cavalry's search for the Kidder party:

> Ef I knowed this young lootenint—I mean Lootenint Kidder. . . . I
> could tell you . . . all you want to know. . . . I have lots uv con-
> fidence in the fightin' sense of Red Bead the Sioux chief, who is
> guidin' the lootenint and his men, and ef that Injun kin have his
> own way thar is a fair show for his guidin' 'em through all right;
> but . . . my experience with you army folks has allus bin that the
> youngsters among ye think they know the most, and this is par-
> ticularly true if they hev just cum from West P'int. . . . I'm told
> that the lootenint we're talkin' about is a new-comer and that this
> is his first scout. Ef that be the case it puts a mighty onsartain look
> on the whole thing.[2]

Kidder was thrice damned by implication: he was a newcomer, he
was on his first scout, and he was from West Point. Never mind that
the facts were otherwise; this was the impression Custer's readers received, and it was hard to rectify. Succeeding writers built on this image
long after Robinson's attempt to set the record straight. James A. Hadley,
described by historian Blaine Burkey as a corporal in Company A,
Eighteenth Kansas, wrote in 1906:

When General Custer learned that Mr. Kidder, the dispatch bearer, was a subaltern in the Second Cavalry, who had been but recently appointed from civil life and was not yet twenty years old, devoid of any sort of military experience, he foresaw a disaster.[3]

Parts of Hadley's tale have an immediacy that suggests either that he was present when the bodies were first discovered, as well as when they were exhumed, or that he was a close confidant of someone who was. Of finding the bodies, he wrote:

> No one in these peaceful days can have any idea of the effect of such sights for the first time on a boy of nineteen—a boy who had never before seen the human body mangled even by accident. . . . There was something in this wanton killing and vile mutilation of these gallant young men . . . that brought tears to the eyes and at the same time aroused every savage instinct.[4]

Of the shirt collar that proved the means of identifying Kidder, Hadley wrote with more detail than others have done:

> After young Kidder's appointment to the army and his assignment to the Second Cavalry had been received, the mother—like all mothers, ever solicitous for her boy's comfort, bought the material for a dozen shirts and made them with her own hands. This material was what used to be called "hickory," and was very strong. This she made stronger by her needlework, every button being "put there for keeps," as the children say. When her boy died, therefore, and the savage fiends undertook to strip him, the shirt-band around the neck refused to give—even the button would not come off—so with a knife the shirt was impatiently cut away and the band left.
>
> This and this only saved the body of young Kidder.[5]

Even author E. A. Brininstool—opinionated, but usually careful—allowed an absurdity to be published in his article on the Kidder massacre for *Hunter-Trader-Trapper* magazine in 1932. For whatever reason, his article indicated that several soldiers in Kidder's detail were under five feet tall. Yet he must have seen the official record of their deaths, for he referred correctly to the soldiers' ages.[6]

In the article, Brininstool could not resist correcting Comstock's grammar and pronunciation as reported by Custer. Lawrence Frost restored Comstock's speech to its original flavor in his 1970 *Westerner*

Monument to Lieutenant Kidder and his men at the battle site. —Photo by Randy Johnson

article.[7] Frost's description of Kidder's last battle relies on the version of George Bent. There is no mention of Kidder's previous experience campaigning against Indians. Frost, however, is able to add a postscript to the story. An avid collector as well as a historian, Frost owned Custer's 1867 field map, and this map played a pivotal role in locating the site of the Kidder fight and the original burial place of the Kidder party.

The western edge of the battlefield is part of the Paul Kuhrt ranch in Sherman County, Kansas, about twenty miles north of Goodland. Thanks to the efforts of Nebraska historian Everette Sutton, aided by Lawrence Frost's writings and Custer's own map, the vicinity of the battle site was reidentified in the 1960s. Early in 1969, the Friends of the Goodland Public Library began a campaign to raise funds for a stone monument at the battle site and a roadside marker on county highway SH28 where it crosses Beaver Creek. With both individual contributions and donations from the historical societies of Cheyenne County

Commemorative marker of Kidder battle on the county highway near Beaver Creek.
—Photo by Randy Johnson

(Kansas) and Dundy County (Nebraska), the group raised the money by midsummer. The two markers were erected and dedicated August 3, 1969, in honor of Lyman Kidder and the men who fell with him 102 years before.

More than three hundred persons attended the dedication ceremony. The Kidder family was represented by Celesta Kidder Adams, whose grandfather, Albert Edward Kidder, was Lyman's cousin and grew up with him in Braintree, Vermont. An old-fashioned community picnic preceded the dedication, followed by an address by U.S. Air Force colonel Ray Sparks of Shawnee Mission, Kansas.[8] Paul Kuhrt hosted the picnic, erected the roadside marker, and introduced the program. The event gave a healing dignity to what had been a place of horror. It proclaims for us that the time for mourning is past, that we need no longer dwell on the tragic deaths of Lyman Kidder and his men, but rather remember the courage and enthusiasm that made them venture forth.

Since then, a plaque has been added to the Kidder party's monument at Fort Leavenworth Cemetery in Kansas, where their bodies were moved after the abandonment of Fort Wallace in 1882. It reads: "Historical research accomplished in 1987 has shown that the remains listed on this monument as 'Unknown Citizen Guide' are those of the Sioux Indian Scout 'Red Bead.'" The plaque was installed July 1, 1987, on the 120th anniversary of the Kidder fight, with appropriate U.S. military and Indian ceremonies. Ron Stover, a Wichita television journalist who had researched the battle, was instrumental in persuading the Veterans' Administration to add Red Bead's name to the monument—where it most assuredly belongs.

Burial monument over mass grave of Lieutenant Kidder's men at Fort Leavenworth. —Photo by Randy Johnson

DESCRIPTIVE LISTS OF DECEASED SOLDIERS OF CO. "M" 2D U.S. CAVALRY BEING THE ESCORT OF LT. KIDDER (LYMAN S.) WHO FELL WITH THEM.

| NAME | RANK | CO. | AGE | HEIGHT | | DESCRIPTION | | | |
				FEET	INCHES	COMPLEXION	EYES	HAIR	
Oscar Close	Sergt.	"M"	23	5	3 3/4	Fair	Brown	Brown	
Charles H. Haynes	Corpl.	"M"	23	5	4 3/4	Dark	Hazel	Brown	
Roger Curry	Private	"M"	23	5	6	Ruddy	Grey	Brown	
Michael Connell	Private	"M"	19	5	7 1/2	Light	Grey	Brown	
William Floyed	Private	"M"	19	5	7	Light	Grey	Dark	
Michael Groman	Private	"M"	19	5	8 1/2	Ruddy	Blue	Dark	
Wm. J. Humphries	Private	"M"	19	5	5	Dark	Hazel	Brown	
Michael Haley	Private	"M"	22	5	8	Dark	Blue	Brown	
Michael Lawler	Private	"M"	21	5	3	Fair	Brown	Sandy	
Charles Teltow	Private	"M"	36	5	3	Fair	Grey	Dark	

Descriptive lists of deceased soldiers of Company M. —Courtesy South Dakota Historical Society

DESCRIPTIVE LISTS OF DECEASED SOLDIERS OF CO. "M" 2D U.S. CAVALRY BEING THE ESCORT OF LT. KIDDER (LYMAN S.) WHO FELL WITH THEM.

NAME	WHERE BORN		OCCUPATION	ENLISTED OR ENROLLED		
	STATE OR KINGDOM	TOWN OR COUNTRY		WHEN	WHERE (TOWN) AND STATE)	BY WHOM
Close	Prussia	Germany	Soldier	Dec. 22d 65	New York, NY	Bvt Lt Col Paulding
Haynes	Maine	Popshen	Clerk	April 16th 66	Boston, Mass	Bvt Col McLaughlin
Curry	Pennsylvania	Chester	Soldier	Sept. 30th 65	Philadelphia, Pa	Lieut Mix
Connell	Ireland	Cork	Laborer	May 8th 66	Boston, Mass	Bvt Col McLaughlin
Floyed	Maryland	Baltimore	Laborer	Sept. 6th 65	Philadelphia, Pa	Lieut Mix
Groman	Maryland	Baltimore	Teamster	May 14th 66	Baltimore, Md	Capt Johnson
Humphries	Ohio	Cincinnati	Laborer	Sept. 2d 65	Cincinnati, Oh	Capt Johnson
Haley	Ireland	Sligo	Boiler Maker	May 8th 66	Boston, Mass	Bvt Col McLaughlin
Lawler	Ireland	Tipparary	Corter	Dec. 1st 66	New York, NY	Capt Gordon
Teltow	Stralsung	Prussia	Soldier	Sept. 2d 65	Cincinnati, Oh	Capt Johnson

South Dakota Historical Society.

Descriptive lists of deceased soldiers of Company M. —Courtesy South Dakota Historical Society

AFTERWORD

I first became interested in the Kidder story shortly after joining the Little Big Horn Associates (LBHA) in 1977. As my collection of Custer-related material grew, the name of Lieutenant Lyman Kidder kept reappearing. The more accounts I read, the more conflicting the information became. I was still trying to uncover the true facts on Kidder and the Kidder massacre when I decided to write this book.

In October 1978 I traveled to St. Paul, Minnesota, to visit the Kidder family plot in Oakland Cemetery and photograph the grave markers. While in town I also visited the Minnesota Historical Society.

The next summer a friend and I drove to the site of the Kidder battle near Goodland, Kansas. With permission from Paul Kuhrt, the owner of the property, we explored the battle site for the first time. It is located

Lyman Kidder's burial monument at Oakland Cemetery.
—Photo by Randy Johnson

in a large valley surrounded by rolling hills; Beaver Creek meanders through the flat basin. Some crops are grown in the area, but much of the land is used for grazing cattle. While there I searched for evidence of the battle, but I came up empty-handed.

I returned to the battlefield in the summer of 1985 along with two fellow researchers. With the aid of metal detectors, we spent three full days exploring the vast area for soldier and Indian artifacts. I was hoping to establish the positions and movements of both sides during the battle. It was not until the third day that I found a small buckle some 250 yards east of the stone memorial. The buckle came from a McClellan saddle, the type used by Kidder and his men.

The following year, while attending a convention of the LBHA in Auburn, New York, I was fortunate enough to meet my coauthor, Nancy Allan. After seeing her enthusiasm for Lieutenant Kidder's story, I asked her to help me develop my research findings into a book. It took us about a year to write the first edition, which we self-published in 1987 under the title *Find Custer! The Kidder Tragedy*. I have continued my research since then and revised the book several times.

In April 1989 I returned to the battle site with another colleague, a scholar of the Custer battle and the American Indian Wars. After several days of exploring the area we found a .44-caliber bullet that was possibly used in the battle. Later that year we visited Big Mound and Dead Buffalo Lake in North Dakota. Lieutenant Kidder fought against Indians at both sites in July 1863.

My colleague and I revisited the battlefield in October 1990. We searched the large ravine believed to be the site of the massacre. The horseshoe-shaped ravine is approximately one hundred yards long and fifty yards wide, with a depth exceeding ten yards at most points. While standing in the bottom of this ravine it is impossible to see anyone approaching from three of its sides; the only view is from the open southern end. Even with the extreme pressure Kidder and his men were under, I find it very doubtful that they would choose this place in which to make their stand. Besides, our hours of searching for artifacts there yielded nothing but trash. We decided to search farther east.

Our quest took us back to the area where in 1985 I had found the only military artifact, the saddle buckle. Within three hundred yards east of the stone marker, we came upon a small ravine, almost a large ditch. In Custer's official report he stated, "They had taken their stand in a dry ditch or ravine about thirty yards in length." This ravine seemed to match Custer's description perfectly. Also, the north end looked exactly like the place shown in an Indian drawing of the massacre that had been recovered after the battle of Summit Springs.

About forty yards northeast of the ravine I recovered a .56/50 Spencer shell casing, the same type of ammunition the Kidder party carried. This was the first evidence that the battle had been fought at this little ravine.

The following year my wife, Jann, and I traveled to California, where we met with Carol Woolfolk, Lyman Kidder's great-niece through Lyman's brother Silas. Woolfolk is the historian of her family and has many family mementos, including a silver tea service that was a wedding gift to Lyman Kidder's parents. She also has several letters Kidder wrote during the Civil War, as well as the cavalry sabre that never reached him at Fort Sedgwick before he left on his fatal mission.

Later the same year I returned to the battle site with my wife and found a loaded .56/56 Spencer cartridge twenty yards southeast of the smaller ravine. We also drove to Benkelman, Nebraska, and located the site of Custer's camp at the forks of the Republican River. The old campsite is southwest of town on private land. There is a large roadside marker southeast of the site on Route 61 telling of Custer's camp and his movements in the area.

Over the next few years, after analyzing the battle site and the artifacts I'd found there, I was able to establish the path that brought Kidder and his men to the ravine in which they made their final stand. Detailed descriptions of the artifacts I recovered appear in the Appendix. From these findings I suggest the following scenario: After being forced off the Wallace Trail, Kidder and his men rode in a southeasterly direction for about half a mile then turned due east. As they passed a point about 75 yards above the ravine, Kidder gave the order to reload, which was no easy task on a moving horse. The result was a trail of dropped pistol and carbine ammunition that extended for over 120 yards. Also along this path were several different types of bullets no doubt fired at the fleeing soldiers by the Indians. Several military buttons in the area indicate that one of the troopers may have been killed or wounded at this point. Perhaps it was the wounding of this soldier that ended the troop's movement to the east. Someone then spotted the ravine below them and they changed direction, heading almost due south to reach it.

Jann Johnson at the roadside marker of Custer's campsite near Benkelman, Nebraska. —Photo by Randy Johnson

Several expended Spencer shell casings about forty yards above the ravine suggest that some of the men provided a covering fire while the rest of them hurried into the ravine, some being wounded in the process.

As the soldiers neared the mouth of the ravine, one of them veered east, either because he lost control of his horse or because he was trying to make his escape that way. He rode across a flat area and then up the side of a hill parallel to the ravine. Before reaching the crest, he fired and ejected a shell casing from his carbine. He came under intense fire as he descended the other side of the hill. He again fired his Spencer, leaving the shell casing along the path, before his horse was shot down. Now on foot, he ran down the rest of the hill as one of the Indians fired as many as twelve shots at him. He was able to fire at least once from his pistol before finally being hit and killed.

Though Kidder and the others were somewhat concealed in the ravine, the Indians soon gained the high ground and poured in a steady rifle

Randy Johnson at the edge of the ravine in which he believes Lieutenant Kidder and his men made their final stand. —Photo by Jann Johnson

fire. As the warriors crept closer, they began using their bows and arrows. About thirty yards west of the ravine the ground slopes downward, which could conceal any Indians who had gathered there. From this position the warriors could arch their arrows upward so that they would drop into the ravine among the soldiers. Many of the Cheyenne circled the troopers' position, firing from their horses. Kidder and his men were able to kill at least two warriors and wound many others before they were overwhelmed. Finally, death came to all except one unfortunate victim who was put to death by the "terrible tortures of fire."[1]

One controversy regarding this battle is the spot that was selected for the burial of these mangled soldiers. When itinerary officer Lieutenant Henry Jackson wrote Judge Kidder that November, he said the bodies were buried about thirty or forty yards north of the creek and about seven hundred yards east of the crossing of the Wallace Trail and Beaver

Creek. Using Lieutenant Jackson's notes, I have surmised that the place of burial was about two hundred yards southeast of the ravine in which I believe Kidder and his men were killed, near where the creek turns back to the north.

The question could be asked, Why would Custer's men bury the bodies such a distance from where they were found? Sergeant James Connelly, who was in charge of the burial party, may have selected the spot for several reasons. First, the command was halted about one-half mile away on the other side of the creek, so the men would have had to carry their shovels and other tools that distance and back, possibly in a wagon. As it was mid-July, the stench from the decomposing bodies of men and horses was undoubtedly overwhelming. Connelly knew it would take time to dig a grave deep and long enough to accommodate twelve bodies, so he'd likely want to stay as far away as feasible until they were finished.

In 1928, Nebraska historian Everette Sutton visited the vicinity of the battle with Charles Carmack. Carmack claimed to have driven the

Beaver Creek, Kansas, as it looks today. —Photo by Randy Johnson

ambulance wagon from Fort Wallace in March of 1868 with the recovery party. Based on Carmack's recollections, Sutton placed the stone marker where it stands today in 1969.[2]

To visit the Kidder battle site, take Route 24 east from Goodland, Kansas, toward Edson. Just before Edson, turn north on county road SH28 for about twelve miles until you see the metal road sign across from the Kuhrt farm. The sign briefly describes the Kidder incident. Continue past the sign for about four hundred yards, crossing Beaver Creek, to the dirt road just after the crossing. This road is very rough, amounting to no more than some ruts through the tall grass. Turn right and follow it for one mile, where you'll find the stone monument honoring Lieutenant Kidder and his men.

Randy Johnson

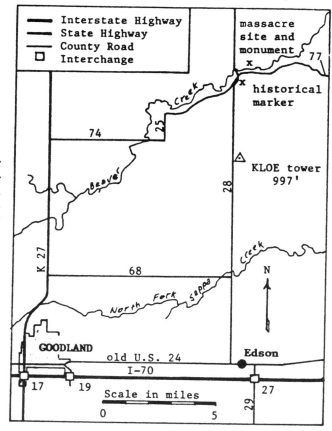

Map to the Kidder battle site. —Courtesy Sherman County Historical Society

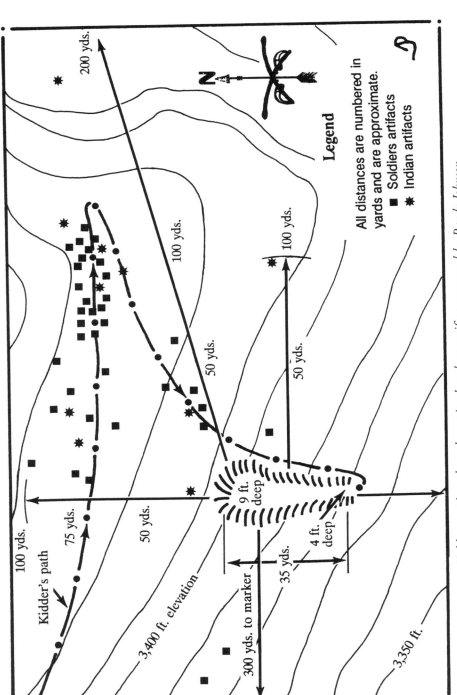

Legend

All distances are numbered in yards and are approximate.

■ Soldiers artifacts

✳ Indian artifacts

200 yds.

100 yds.

100 yds.

50 yds.

50 yds.

100 yds.

50 yds.

Kidder's path

75 yds.

100 yds.

50 yds.

3,400 ft. elevation

9 ft. deep

4 ft. deep

35 yds.

300 yds. to marker

3,350 ft.

N

Kidder party's path to the ravine based on artifacts recovered by Randy Johnson.

APPENDIX: ARTIFACTS

The following pages are photos of artifacts recovered by Randy Johnson, most from the Kidder battle site, as well as some from Big Mound and Dead Buffalo Lake.

Among the finds were large quantities of .56/50 Spencer carbine and .44-caliber Remington pistol ammunition. Most of the unfired Spencer cartridges that were originally dropped during the Kidder battle had come apart, due to minerals in the soil reacting with the gunpowder inside the loaded shell and causing corrosion. While eroded shells were very common at the Kidder site, several Spencer cartridges were found intact. Remington cartridges, however, had a heavy paper backing that contained the gunpowder. As the paper and powder charge dissolved over the years, only the lead .44-caliber bullet remained.

I found no evidence of misfires in any of the ammunition I recovered at the battle site. All the .56/50 cartridges were of the same manufacture, Jacob Goldmark, and all had the head stamp *J.G.*; one .56/56 Spencer cartridge, found southeast of the ravine, had no head stamp at all.

I also recovered Indian ammunition of various calibers, both fired and dropped. The main weapon of the Plains Indian at the time was the bow and arrow, although by then most arrow points were manufactured by white men. The Indians usually traded or bought these arrowheads, which were made of iron and punched out on presses, at forts and trading posts. Some Indians did make their own points, using barrel hoops or other metal stock and chiseling them into shape. I recovered no complete iron arrow points in this study. The arrows may have disintegrated over the years from the minerals in the ground. I found one stone arrow point at the Kidder site, but it is doubtful it was used in the battle.

I recovered eight military buttons at the site, two eagle uniform buttons and six iron trouser buttons. The first eagle button was Civil War style, from a four-button sack coat or a fatigue blouse. This brass-lined button was back-marked *Waterbury Button Co.* The second eagle button was smaller, as from a uniform cuff or the strap of a forage cap; this button was back-stamped *Scovills & Co. Extra.* I also found the top half of a cavalry cross-saber insignia, which would have been worn on a forage cap. The other half probably remained on the cap and was carried from the battle site by an Indian.

No artifacts were found in the ravine. Anything that may still be there is either buried too deep to be detected or was washed down to Beaver Creek by one of the many floods over the last 120 years. I found no evidence of previous metal detection in the area. Some of the cartridges I found were torn in half, having been struck by some object, probably a plow blade. The owner of the property confirmed that at one time the site had been plowed for crops. The area is presently used as pasture land, and cattle graze there.

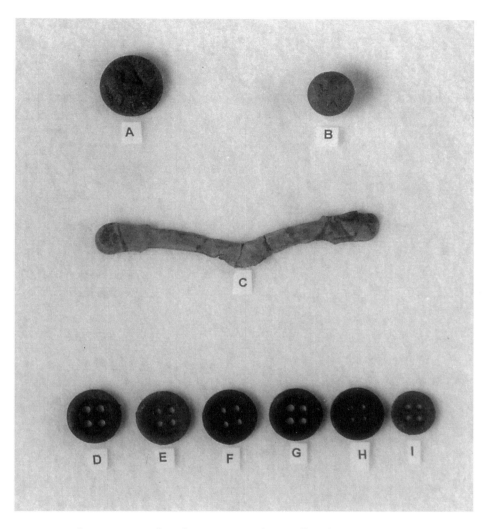

Personal items: A. uniform button; B. uniform cuff or forage-cap button; C. top half of a cavalry cross-saber insignia; D.–I. iron two-piece trouser buttons.

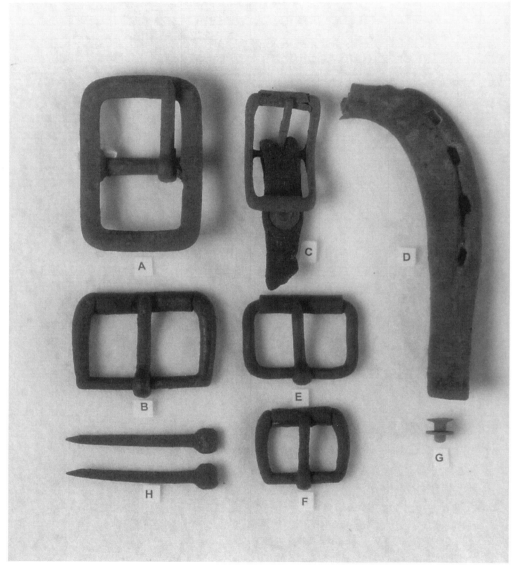

Horse-related items: A. pattern 1859-7A buckle for a halter near cheek ring or hitching strap McClellan saddle; B. pattern 1859-4A roller buckle for girth or surcingle McClellan saddle; C. pattern 1859-10A roller buckle bridle head stall McClellan saddle (recovered at Dead Buffalo Lake); D. broken cavalry horseshoe. E.–F. pattern 1859 roller buckles McClellan saddle; G. saddle or accouterment rivet; H. horseshoe nails.

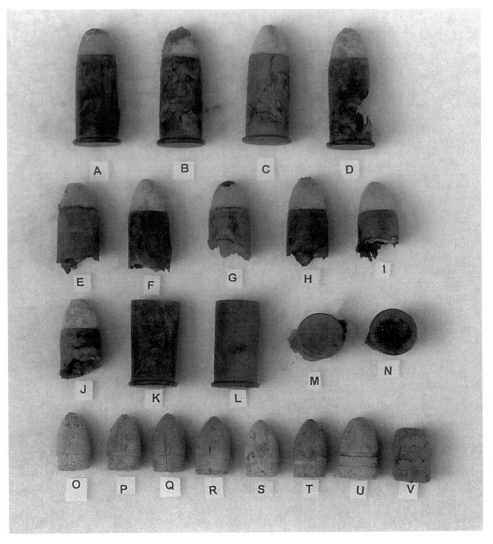

Army pistol and carbine ammunition: A.–D. intact loaded .56/50 Spencer cartridges; E.-J. damaged loaded .56/50 Spencer cartridges; K.–L. .56/50 Spencer cartridge casings; M.–N. backs of Spencer cartridges; O.–T. unfired .44 Remington pistol bullets; U.–V. fired .56/50 Spencer bullets.

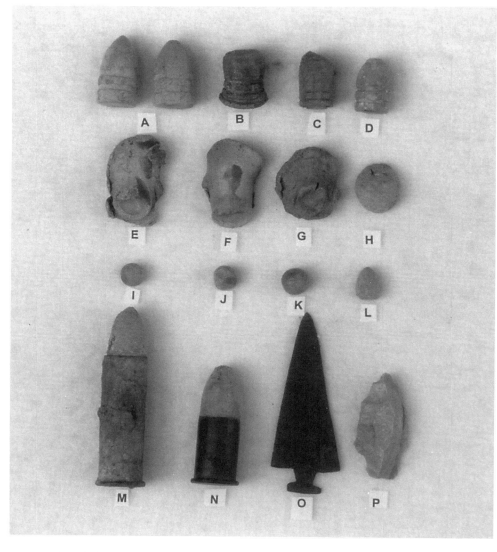

Indian bullets and arrowheads: A. .52 Sharps percussion carbine bullets; B. .58 bullet from a rim-fire M1865 Springfield rifle (First Allin conversion); C. fired .44 Henry bullet; D. .44 bullet, possibly a Volcanic; E.–G. high-impact bullets, possibly Sharps; H.–J. various caliber musket balls; K. .36 round ball for a percussion revolver; L. .31 conical ball for an M1848 Colt pocket revolver; M. loaded .50/ 70 centerfire cartridge, Berdan primed, U.M.C. Co.; N. loaded .56/56 Spencer cartridge; O. iron arrowhead (recovered at Big Mound); P. stone arrowhead.

Notes

I. "When the Watchword Is Victory or Death"

1. Minnie Dubbs Millbrook, "The West Breaks in General Custer," *Kansas Historical Quarterly* 36 (Summer 1970): 122. Custer's role in the Hancock campaign, of which this scout formed a part, is well known to Custer students. More information on the subject can be found under Frost in the bibliography.
2. George Armstrong Custer, *My Life on the Plains*, ed. Milo Milton Quaife (Lincoln: University of Nebraska Press, 1966), 192–93.
3. Ibid., 195–200.

II. Beginnings

1. Jefferson P. Kidder Family Papers, South Dakota Historical Society, Pierre, S. Dak.
2. Morgan H. Stafford, *A Genealogy of the Kidder Family* (Rutland, Vt.: Tuttle, 1941), xxxi.
3. H. Royce Bass, *The History of Braintree, Vermont* (Rutland, Vt.: Tuttle, 1883), 157.
4. *Biographical Directory of the American Congress, 1774–1971* (Washington D.C.: Government Printing Office, 1971), 1231.
5. Stafford, *Genealogy*, 262.
6. J. Fletcher Williams, *A History of the City of Saint Paul to 1875* (St. Paul: Minnesota Historical Society Press, 1983; first published in 1876 by the Minnesota Historical Society as vol. 4 of the *Collections of the Minnesota Historical Society*), 467.
7. *Memorial of the Legislative Assembly of Dakota Asking the Admission of Jefferson P. Kidder to a Seat in the House of Representatives.* 36th Cong., 1st sess., 1859, Mis. Doc. 73.
8. George W. Kingsbury, *History of Dakota Territory*, vol. 1 (Chicago: S. J. Clarke, 1915), 102–3.
9. Williams, *Saint Paul*, 396.
10. Ibid., 398.

III. "The Noble Work of Putting Down Rebellion"

1. Kidder Papers.
2. Iowa General Assembly, *Roster and Record of Iowa Soldiers in the War of the Rebellion*, vol. 4 (Des Moines, 1910), 847.
3. Lyman Kidder's letters home, Carol Woolfolk collection, San Jacinto, Calif.
4. Kidder Papers.
5. Eugene M. Wilson, "Narrative of the First Regiment of Mounted Rangers," in *Minnesota in the Civil and Indian Wars, 1861–1865* (St. Paul: Pioneer Press, 1891), 520.
6. Wilson, "Narrative," 521–22.
7. *The War of the Rebellion: A Compilation of the Official Records of the Union and Confederate Armies* (Washington D.C.: Government Printing Office, 1888–1901), I, XXII, pt. 1, 367.
8. Wilson, "Narrative," 522–23.
9. *The War of the Rebellion,* I, XXII, pt. 1, 369.
10. Wilson, "Narrative," 520–21.
11. Ibid., 522–23.
12. Kidder Papers.
13. Doane Robinson, "Lieut. Lyman S. Kidder and the Tragedy on Beaver Creek," *Monthly South Dakotan* 4 (November 1901): 208.

IV. Officer's Call

1. This and all letters following that relate to Lyman Kidder's appointment are from the Kidder Papers.
2. General Services Administration, National Archives Records Services, Washington D.C.
3. Ibid.
4. *Yankton Union and Dakotian*, 15 June 1867, quoted in John S. Gray, "The Kidder Massacre," *Westerners Brand Book* 19, no. 6 (August 1962): 41.

V. "Uncommonly Dear as a Companion and Friend"

1. Alfred Elliott Bates, "Personal Recollections—Post Bellum," in *From Everglade to Canon with the Second Dragoons (Second United States Cavalry) 1836–1875,* comp. Theophilus Francis Rodenbough (New York: Van Nostrand, 1875), 379.

2. All correspondence between the Kidder family members, and between Custer, Sherman, and others and Jefferson Kidder, is from the Kidder Papers.

3. William H. Bisbee, *Through Four American Wars* (Boston: Meador, 1931), 188–89.

4. *Message of the President of the United States and Accompanying Documents to the Two Houses of Congress,* 40th Cong., 2nd sess., 1867, Ex. Doc. 1, 35. Report of the Secretary of War.

5. Lawrence A. Frost, *The Court-Martial of General George Armstrong Custer* (Norman: University of Oklahoma Press, 1968), 14–15.

6. Millbrook, "West," 128.

7. Robinson, "Kidder," 207–9.

8. Millbrook, "West," 127.

9. Custer, *My Life*, 200.

10. G. A. Custer to Lieutenant T. B. Weir, 7 August 1867, in the Kidder Papers.

11. Custer, *My Life*, 197. "When within a mile of the stream, I observed several buzzards floating lazily in circles to the left of our trail." Lt. Jackson: "Their trail veered 1/2 mile and there we found Lt. Kidder and eleven men."

12. Theodore Davis, "A Summer on the Plains," *Harper's New Monthly Magazine* 36 (February 1868), 306.

13. Ibid., 306–7.

14. Custer, *My Life*, 198.

15. George Bent, "Forty Years with the Cheyennes," *The Frontier* 4 (February 1906), 4–5.

VI. A Father's Pilgrimage

1. Custer, 7 August 1867 report to the acting adjutant general, National Archives Records Services, Washington D.C.

2. Custer, *My Life*, 201.

3. Kingsbury, *Dakota*, 602–3.

4. Frost, *Court-Martial*, 262–63.

5. Ibid., 165–74, 197–98.

6. Lieutenant Henry Jackson, itinerary of the march of the U.S. Seventh Cavalry, entry for 12 July 1867, Lawrence A. Frost Collection, Monroe Library, Monroe, Mich.

7. Theodore R. Davis, "A Summer on the Plains," *Harper's Monthly Magazine*, February 1868: 300.

8. All Beecher letters are from *A Memorial to Frederick H. Beecher*, a pamphlet prepared by his parents, the Reverend Charles and Sarah Beecher, Portland, Maine, 1870.

9. John S. Gray, "New Light on Will Comstock, Kansas Scout," in *Custer and His Times*, vol. 1 (El Paso: Little Big Horn Associates, 1981), 203–4.

10. George A. Forsyth, "Beecher Island Battle," *Harper's New Monthly Magazine*, June 1895: 127.

VII. Homecoming

1. This letter repeats Judge Kidder's error of placing Beaver Creek in Colorado instead of Kansas.

2. Howard Roberts Lamar, *Dakota Territory, 1861–1869: A Study of Frontier Politics* (New Haven: Yale University Press, 1956), 114–16.

3. Kingsbury, *Dakota*, 931–36.

4. Ibid., 936–37.

5. Robinson, "Kidder," 208; *Historical Atlas of Dakota* (Chicago: A. T. Andreas/R. R. Donnelly & Sons, 1884), 103.

6. "Death of Judge Kidder," *Saint Paul and Minneapolis Pioneer Press*, 3 October 1883, 7.

VIII. Remembrance

1. Robinson, "Kidder," 208.

2. Custer, *My Life*, 189–90. Minnie Millbrook points out that if Custer had followed orders and used Sedgwick as his supply base instead of Wallace, Kidder probably would not have died (Millbrook, "West," 134).

3. James A. Hadley, "The Opening Tragedy: Death of Lieut. Kidder," *The Farm and Home Sentinel* (photocopy; probably Indianapolis, 1906): 2.

4. Hadley, "Tragedy," 3.

5. Ibid., 3.

6. E. A. Brininstool, "The Kidder Massacre," *Hunter-Trader-Trapper* 65 (December 1932): 12.

7. Lawrence A. Frost, "Custer and the Kidder Massacre," *Westerner* (September 1970): 55.

8. Frost: "Kidder," 57; *Benkelman (Nebraska) Post*, 22 July 1969; *Colby* (Kansas) *Prairie Drummer*, 17 July and 3 August 1969; *Goodland* (Kansas) *Daily News*, 4 August 1969.

Afterword
1. Custer, *My Life,* 198.
2. Everette Sutton, letter to Mr. Green, 15 July 1954, Lawrence A. Frost collection, Monroe Library, Monroe, Mich.

BIBLIOGRAPHY

Books and Articles

Anderson, Gary Clayton. *Little Crow: Spokesman for the Sioux*. Saint Paul: Minnesota Historical Society Press, 1986.

Andrist, Ralph K. "Massacre!" *American Heritage* 13 (April 1962): 8–17, 108–11.

Athearn, Robert G. *William Tecumseh Sherman and the Settlement of the West*. Norman: University of Oklahoma Press, 1956.

Bass, H. Royce. *The History of Braintree, Vermont*. Rutland, Vt.: Tuttle, 1883.

Bates, Alfred Elliott. "Personal Recollections—Post Bellum." In *From Everglade to Canon with the Second Dragoons (Second United States Cavalry) 1836–1875*. Comp. Theophilus Francis Rodenbough. New York: D. Van Nostrand, 1875.

Beecher, Charles and Sarah. *A Memorial to Frederick H. Beecher*. Pamphlet. Portland, Maine: 1870.

Bent, George. "Forty Years with the Cheyennes." *The Frontier* 4 (February 1906): 4–5.

Biographical Directory of the American Congress, 1774–1971. Washington D.C.: Government Printing Office, 1971.

Bisbee, William H. *Through Four American Wars*. Boston: Meador, 1931.

Brininstool, E. A. "The Kidder Massacre." *Hunter-Trader-Trapper* 65 (December 1932): 12–14, 18.

Burkey, Blaine. *Custer, Come at Once!* Hays, Kans.: Author, 1976.

Chronology and Documentary Handbook of the State of Minnesota. Dobbs Ferry, N.Y.: Oceana, 1978.

Chronology and Documentary Handbook of the State of Vermont. Dobbs Ferry, N.Y.: Oceana, 1979.

Custer, George Armstrong. *My Life on the Plains.* Ed. Milo Milton Quaife. Lincoln: University of Nebraska Press, 1966.

Danziger, Edmund Jefferson. *The Chippewa of Lake Superior.* Norman: University of Oklahoma Press, 1979.

Davis, Theodore. "A Summer on the Plains." *Harper's New Monthly Magazine* 36 (February 1868): 292–307.

Dictionary of American Biography. New York: Scribner, 1963.

Dornbusch, C. E., comp. *Military Bibliography of the Civil War.* 3 vols. New York: New York Public Library and Arno Press, 1971.

Ellis, Richard N. *General Pope and U.S. Indian Policy.* Albuquerque: University of New Mexico, 1970.

Ellis, William A. *Norwich University: Her History, Her Graduates, Her Roll of Honor.* Concord, N.H.: Rumford, 1898.

Encyclopedia Britannica. 1968 ed., s.v. "Minnesota."

Folwell, William Watts. *Minnesota, the North Star State.* Boston: Houghton Mifflin, 1908. Reprint, New York: AMS Press, 1973.

Forsyth, George A. "Beecher Island Battle." *Harper's New Monthly Magazine* (June 1895).

Frost, Lawrence A. *The Court-Martial of General George Armstrong Custer.* Norman: University of Oklahoma Press, 1968.

———. "Custer and the Kidder Massacre." *Westerner* (September 1970): 26–29, 55–57.

Gray, John S. "New Light on Will Comstock, Kansas Scout." In *Custer and His Times.* vol. 1, 183–207. El Paso: Little Big Horn Associates, 1981.

———, comp. "The Kidder Massacre: The Tragedy on Beaver Creek, Kansas, in 1867, as Told in Contemporary News Dispatches." *The Westerners Brand Books* (Chicago) 19 (August 1962): 41–42.

Grinnell, George Bird. *The Fighting Cheyennes.* Norman: University of Oklahoma Press, 1955.

Hadley, James A. "The Opening Tragedy: Death of Lieut. Kidder." *The Farm and Home Sentinel* (October 15, 1906): 2, 3.

Hart, Herbert M. *Old Forts of the Northwest.* New York: Bonanza Books, 1963.

Heitman, Francis B. *Historical Register and Dictionary of the United States Army.* 2 vols. Washington, D.C.: Government Printing Office, 1903.

Historical Atlas of Dakota. Chicago: A. T. Andreas/R. R. Donnelley & Sons, 1884.

Holmquist, June Drenning, and Jean A. Brookins. *Minnesota's Major Historic Sites: A Guide.* 2nd ed. St. Paul: Minnesota Historical Society, 1972.

Illustrated Historical Atlas of the State of Minnesota. Chicago: A. T. Andreas, 1874.

Indians in Minnesota. St. Paul: League of Women Voters of Minnesota, 1971.

Iowa General Assembly. *Roster and Record of Iowa Soldiers in the War of the Rebellion.* Des Moines, 1910.

Kingsbury, George W. *History of Dakota Territory.* 5 vols. Chicago: S. J. Clarke, 1915.

Kunz, Virginia Brainard. *Muskets to Missiles: A Military History of Minnesota.* St. Paul: Minnesota Statehood Centennial Commission, 1958.

Lamar, Howard R. *Dakota Territory, 1861–1889: A Study of Frontier Politics.* New Haven: Yale University Press, 1956.

Millbrook, Minnie Dubbs. "The West Breaks in General Custer." *Kansas Historical Quarterly* 36 (Summer 1970): 113–148.

Minnesota in the Civil and Indian Wars, 1861–1865. 2nd ed. St. Paul: Pioneer Press Company, 1891.

Montgomery, Mrs. Frank C. "Fort Wallace and Its Relation to the Frontier." *Kansas Historical Collections* 17 (1928): 189–283.

Nash, C. W. "Narrative of Hatch's Independent Battalion of Cavalry." In *Minnesota in the Civil and Indian Wars, 1861–1865.* St. Paul: Pioneer Press, 1891.

Oehler, C. M. *The Great Sioux Uprising.* New York: Oxford University Press, 1959.

Robinson, Doane. "Lieut. Lyman S. Kidder and the Tragedy on Beaver Creek." *Monthly South Dakotan* 4 (November 1901): 207–14.

Rodenbough, Theophilus Francis, comp. *From Everglade to Canon with the Second Dragoons (Second United States Cavalry) 1836–1875.* New York: D. Van Nostrand, 1875.

Stafford, Morgan H. *A Genealogy of the Kidder Family.* Rutland, Vt.: Tuttle, 1941.

Utley, Robert M. *The Indian Frontier of the American West, 1846–1890.* Albuquerque: University of New Mexico, 1984.

Voight, Barton R. "The Death of Lyman S. Kidder." *South Dakota History* 6 (Winter 1975): 1–32.

The War of the Rebellion: A Compilation of the Official Records of the Union and Confederate Armies. Washington, D.C.: Government Printing Office, 1888–1901.

Werner, Fred H. *Heroic Fort Sedgwick and Julesburg: A Study in Courage.* Greeley, Colo.: Werner Publications, 1987.

Williams, J. Fletcher. *A History of the City of Saint Paul to 1875.* St. Paul: Minnesota Historical Society Press, 1983. First published in 1876 by the Minnesota Historical Society as vol. 4 of *Collections of the Minnesota Historical Society.*

Wilson, Eugene M. "Narrative of the First Regiment of Mounted Rangers." In *Minnesota in the Civil and Indian Wars, 1861–1865.* St. Paul: Pioneer Press, 1891.

Public Documents and Manuscript Collections

Kidder Family Papers. Carol Woolfolk collection, San Jacinto, Calif.

Kidder, Jefferson P., Family Papers. South Dakota State Historical Society, Pierre, S. Dak.

National Archives. Military and Pensions Records: Edward Lyon Bailey, Charles Brewster, Avery Billings Cain, Hiram Latham, John Mix.

National Archives. Returns from U.S. Military Posts: Fort Abercrombie, Fort Snelling, Fort Wallace.

U.S. Congress. House. *Memorial of the Legislative Assembly of Dakota Asking the Admission of Jefferson P. Kidder to a Seat in the House of Representatives.* 36th Cong., 1st sess., 1859. Mis. Doc. 73.

U.S. Congress. House. *Message of the President of the United States and Accompanying Documents to the Two Houses of Congress.* 40th Cong., 2nd sess., 1867. Ex. Doc. 1. Report of the Secretary of War.

Newspapers

Benkelman (Nebraska) *Post.*

Colby (Kansas) *Prairie Drummer.*

Goodland (Kansas) *Daily News.*

Saint Paul and Minneapolis Pioneer Press.

Saint Paul Daily Press.

Saint Paul Pioneer.

INDEX

117

ABOUT THE AUTHORS

As a member of the Little Big Horn Associates and the Custer Battle-field Historical and Museum Association, **Randy Johnson** is an active student of the Custer enigma. Born in Chicago, Mr. Johnson served with the army in Vietnam and afterward attended Harper College in Palatine, Illinois. He currently works for the U.S. Postal Service and lives in Palatine.

Since joining the Little Big Horn Associates in 1976, **Nancy P. Allan** has published several articles on Custer's life and times. Born a West Virginian, Ms. Allan has lived in Illinois since 1953. She is an alumna of Morris Harvey College and the University of Michigan. Ms. Allan retired in 1995 after sixteen years as a reference librarian at the Barrington Area Library in Barrington, Illinois. She lives in Hoffman Estates, Illinois.

A Dispatch to Custer was originally self-published under the title *Find Custer! The Kidder Tragedy,* and was a winner of the Little Big Horn Associates Literary Award.

We encourage you to patronize your local bookstore. Most stores will order any title that they do not stock. You may also order directly from Mountain Press using the order form provided below or by calling our toll-free number and using your VISA or MasterCard. We will gladly send you a catalog upon request.

Some other titles of interest:

_____ THE BLOODY BOZEMAN
     The Perilous Trail to Montana's Gold $16.00, paper

_____ CHIEF JOSEPH AND THE NEZ PERCES
     A Photographic History $15.00, paper

_____ CHILDREN OF THE FUR TRADE
     Forgotten Métis of the Pacific Northwest $15.00, paper

_____ LAKOTA NOON
     The Indian Narrative of Custer's Defeat $36.00, cloth $18.00, paper

_____ LEWIS AND CLARK
     A Photographic Journey $18.00, paper

_____ THE JOURNALS OF PATRICK GASS
     Members of the Lewis and Clark Expedition $36.00, cloth $20.00, paper

_____ THE MYSTERY OF E TROOP
     Custer's Gray Horse Company at the Little Bighorn $18.00, paper

_____ THE PIIKANI BLACKFEET
     A Culture Under Siege $30.00, cloth $18.00, paper

_____ WILLIAM HENRY JACKSON
     Framing the Frontier $36.00, cloth $22.00, paper

Please include $3.00 per order to cover postage and handling.

Please send the books marked above. I've enclosed $_____

Name_____

Address_____

City_____State_____Zip_____

☐ Payment enclosed (check or money order in U.S. funds)

Bill my: ☐ VISA   ☐ MasterCard Expiration Date:_____

Card No._____

Signature_____

MOUNTAIN PRESS PUBLISHING COMPANY
P.O. Box 2399 • Missoula, MT 59806
Order Toll-Free 1-800-234-5308
Have your MasterCard or Visa ready.